THIS AIR FRYER BOOK IS NOT A COOKBOOK

BASIC EDUCATION FOR BEGINNERS WHO WANT TO
OWN AN AIR FRYER & AIR FRYER OWNERS WHO
NEVER OPENED THE BOX

NICOLE R. STEWART

CONTENTS

Free Gift!!!

Included with your purchase of this book is my 7 Free Air Fryer Recipes.
In your free gift you will learn:

- A brief recap on what an air fryer is
- 5 useful tips before using an air fryer
- FREE simple recipes to start using with your air fryer

Visit the link below to receive your free gift in your email

Go to https://nicolerstewart.com/free-recipes

or scan the code below to claim your free recipes!

INTRODUCTION

Life gets busy, especially when you have to deal with office meetings and other obligations, then come back home and deal with family duties. You need a convenient cooking device that helps you save time. If you own an air fryer or are thinking about buying one, this air fryer book is for you. It will provide you with a foundational understanding of an air fryer before you purchase an air fryer or cookbook. An air fryer is the newest and best way to cook without oil or added fat. By owning one, you don't have to spend extra money on restaurants or eat food with no nutrients. If you are looking for a healthy way to prepare food and improve your health, then you are in the right place. If you already own an air fryer that you received as a gift, but you never opened the box because you have no idea how to use it properly, then this book is also for you.

If you are a beginner cook and want to surprise your family and friends with more fresh, delicious meal options at the table, then you need this book. This is your go-to guide for the air fryer. Owning a comprehensive guide is as important as buying your first air fryer. If you want to acquire all the secrets and learn how to prepare the most delicious meals, then this book is for you. Are you tired and frustrated with a stove? Of frying in oil and having to clean the splatters in a hot kitchen after using the stovetop or oven? Well, forget about it. The air fryer is a more accessible alternative. You can use it to stir-fry, sauté, steam, simmer, bake, and so much more. Compared to an oven, an air fryer cooks food in half the time, and prepares crispy, delicious meals without cups of oil. You need an air fryer if you want to enjoy a wide variety of tasty meals.

Air fryers allow you to cook almost anything. You can use it to cook meat, fish, poultry, vegetables, fruit, and a wide variety of desserts. In this guide, you will find all the information you need to become an air fryer expert. Ideal for new and experienced owners alike, this all-inclusive guide shows you how to use all the core functions so you can create a wide variety of family-friendly meals. This book also provides care and maintenance tips as well as professional advice so you can get the best out of your device. This essential air fryer book will increase your cooking desire and skills in no time. It will motivate you to cook mouth-watering dishes and help you enjoy the art of cooking. It will show you how to properly use the air fryer and save time in the kitchen. This air fryer book is the perfect companion for home cooks. However, this is not a cookbook. It is your all-inclusive kitchen companion that discusses everything about the air fryer and helps you get the most from your new appliance.

My name is Nicole Stewart, and I am an experienced cook and up-and-coming writer in the cooking, food, and wine niche with a passion to help others who are new to air frying understand its benefits. I am also an expert on health and nutrition. Over the years, being an experienced person in these topics helped me to understand the connection between healthy eating and the human body. Every day my current goal is to help people achieve their weight-loss targets and still have fun in the kitchen. I am passionate about nutrition, dieting, and healthy living, and am an avid fan of the popular air fryer cooking appliance.

In recent years I have been using an air fryer for most of my cooking and have lost over 40 pounds by eating meals made with an air fryer. I genuinely love cooking for my family and friends and regularly use the air fryer for most of the meals during visits and gatherings. This book can assist readers to safely and effectively achieve their weight loss goals by effectively using an air fryer. When I'm not in the kitchen or writing, I enjoy walking on the beach, listening to music, and reading a variety of books written by different authors. I currently reside in the state of Maryland. Enjoy your copy of *This Air Fryer Book Is NOT a Cookbook!*

1

AIR FRYER 101

An air fryer is a modern-day kitchen appliance that is the direct counterpart of the old-style oven, frying pan, and multicooker. Although the device is not new and has been around for some years, it has gone viral. According to the market research firm NPD Group, approximately 40% of U.S. homes have one. With an air fryer, you use hot air instead of oil to cook your meals.

An air fryer allows you to use up to 80% less fat. You can use an it to roast, bake, grill, and fry foods. An air fryer heats the air to a temperature of around 400°F. The hot air constantly circulates through the pan and around the food at high speed. This method of cooking gives the food a crispy outer layer. This way, your dishes cook evenly on all sides with a crispy crust.

The air fryer offers low-fat options of food that would usually be cooked in a deep fryer. As a result, ordinarily unhealthy foods such as fried chicken, onion rings, and French fries, are cooked with no oil or up to 80% less fat content than conventional cooking methods. Cooking with an air fryer ensures that you get healthier cooked food. This method ensures that you get healthier foods while still enjoying the quality, texture, and crunchiness you desire.

By circulating hot air quickly and evenly around foods in the cooking chamber, the food is soft and moist inside and dry and crispy on the outside. An air fryer can be used for pretty much everything.

Rapid Air Technology is the technology used for cooking food inside the air fryer. This method cooks the food with hot air instead of oil. You can enjoy fried fish, chicken, beef, chips, pastries, and more. The cooking chamber of the air fryer heats the food efficiently. An exhaust fan placed above the food chamber provides the required airflow, which allows the hot air to circulate around the food constantly and cook it. The circulated hot air also cooks the food more evenly.

An air fryer is similar to a countertop convection oven, but with modifications. The air fryer has a fan that circularly blows hot air in the cooking chamber. Again, this ensures even cooking and a crisp crust. The food is placed in a perforated basket, which allows more exposure to hot moving air. Another big difference is that most air fryers today are small, which means there is less room inside, so the heat intensifies and less cooking time is needed.

AIR FRYER PARTS

Air fryers have three essential parts.

- The air fryer base: The base is the air fryer's main component.
- The basket: The basket holds the food. Depending on the brand and model, it has round holes or a mesh base so air can circulate easily.
- The basket base: This is the bottom part of the air fryer that holds the basket. This part catches crumbs and oil that fall through the basket's holes.

An oven-style air fryer has the oven as the central unit. It looks like a convection oven with a cooking tray, racks, and basket.

Control panel

The control panel is where you set the time and temperature to cook food.

What can you do with an air fryer?

- You can use this device to cook deep-fried foods (chicken fingers, onion rings, and French fries). However, you can also cook foods that are usually cooked in a microwave or oven (such as pork loin, baked potatoes, pizza, pastries, or calzone).
- You can use it to sauté or grill foods (vegetables, fish, chicken, steak, pork chops, and others).
- You can reheat food with this cooking device.
- You can prepare ingredients with this appliance, such as cooking bacon for sandwiches, roasting peppers for pasta, or toasting nuts for a salad.

The benefits of the air fryer

1. Less heat: Your kitchen gets warmer when you cook foods in your oven, especially during summer days. If you live in a small apartment, then it is a problem. Cooking with an air fryer means less heat, therefore, no problem.
2. It is versatile: With an air fryer, you can air fry, grill, roast, and bake your food. Most manufacturers offer

optional accessories such as grill pans and nonstick baking pans, which help you cook almost anything in your air fryer.

3. Better than other appliances: The air fryer is more effective than the microwave, oven, deep fryer, and dehydrator. The air fryer replaces all these devices and can quickly cook up perfect dishes for every meal without sacrificing flavor.

4. It is healthier: An air fryer uses a convection process to cook foods. This process results in less oil and fewer calories and still seals in flavor, and produces a crisp, crunchy texture.

5. Convenient: The air fryer is compact enough to fit neatly on a countertop, and it takes up considerably less space than larger cooking appliances that do much less.

6. Cook faster: With an air fryer, food takes less time to cook than if cooked in a conventional oven. Many air fryers also have built-in presets, so controlling the exact cook times and temperatures is simple.

7. Calorie reduction: One of the main benefits of an air fryer is that it helps you eat low-calorie food. When deep frying food in oil, you add many calories. The reduction of extra calories is also a significant key to a successful diet.

8. Reduction of energy expenditure: You can use up to 50% less energy when using the air fryer.

9. Saving money: Purchase less oil for cooking and save energy costs when cooking with the air fryer.

10. Great for frozen foods: The air fryer is great for frozen foods such as egg rolls, fish sticks, and French fries.

11. Ease of cleaning: The air fryer is very easy to clean. Most of the air fryer parts that come into contact with food are dishwasher-safe.

12. Safe and easy to use: Being around a pot of hot oil can be dangerous. Air fryers remove this danger entirely. You wouldn't need to worry about burned skin from hot oil spillage with your air fryer.

13. No guesswork: Most air fryers have automatic cooking functions, so there is no guesswork. Depending on the model you choose, you can cook various foods with just a press of a button. The machine controls the cooking times and cooking temperatures.

14. It is portable: The air fryer quart model is a perfect travel companion. It takes up very little space and you can heat up or prepare a quick and delicious meal while on the road.

Essential Accessories

Here are some of the standard accessories:

1. The cake barrel: This can be either round or square, and is nonstick. It is also used for egg dishes, casseroles, and desserts.

2. The grill pan: The grill pan is a nonstick addition that can be substituted for the air fryer's basket. It is used for grilling meat, vegetables, and fish.

3. The rack: This round metal rack allows you to add a second layer of food to the air fryer. You can use it for cooking lightweight foods like bacon.

4. The pizza pan: You can cook pizzas with it. You can also bake pancakes, giant cookies, and biscuits with it.

5. The silicone liners: They are great for muffins, mini meatloaves, cupcakes, on-the-go frittatas, and small quick breads.

6. The skewer rack: You can cook vegetables and meat shish kebabs with it.

Accessory removal

Cooking with a pot in an appliance is an excellent idea. However, you need to be able to remove the cooking dish insert with ease. You need:

1. Silicone-tipped or wooden tongs are a good choice for air frying. Most air fryer baskets and accessories are nonstick. A pair of nonmetal tongs help to flip oversized food items such as egg rolls.

2. Heat-resistant mini mitts or pinch mitts are especially helpful when lifting racks, pots, and barrels. They are more heat resistant and less unwieldy than traditional oven mitts.

Managing your air fryer

- Place the air fryer on a level and heatproof kitchen countertop. If you have granite surfaces, this is perfect.
- Avoid putting it close to the wall as this will dissipate the heat causing slower cooking times. Make sure there is at least 5 to 6 inches of space between the air fryer and the wall.
- Oven-safe baking sheets and cake pans may be used in the air fryer as long as they can fit inside easily and the door can close.

Before cooking

- Always preheat your air fryer before cooking.
- Use a hand-pumped spray bottle for applying the oil. Adopting this method will cause you to use less oil and is an easier option than brushing or drizzling.
- Always bread your food if it is required. Press the breading firmly onto the vegetable or meat so the crumbs do not fall off easily.

While cooking

- Before cooking, add water to the air fryer drawer to prevent excessive smoke and heat when cooking high-fat foods. Use this technique when cooking bacon, burgers, sausages, and similar foods.

- Secure light foods such as bread slices with toothpicks so they do not blow around.
- Avoid putting too many food items into the air fryer basket. If you overcrowd the basket, the food will not cook properly. Also, the food will not be crispy.
- Shaking the fryer or flipping the food halfway through the cooking time is recommended. It will make sure that everything inside cooks evenly.
- Opening the air fryer a few times to check how the food is doing won't affect the cooking time, so do not worry.

When cooking is complete

- First, remove the basket from the drawer. Then, remove the food to prevent the oil from remaining on what you just fried.
- The remaining liquids in the air fryer drawer can be used to make delicious marinades and sauces. If you find it too greasy, you can always reduce it in a saucepan to eliminate the excess liquid.
- Cleaning both the basket and drawer after every use is imperative.

Tips for air fryer success

1. Know your appliance: First, read the appliance manual because air fryers are not created equal. Parts of some air fryers are dishwasher-safe, but you have to hand-wash others. Remember, any misuse of your air fryer or its components could void the warranty. Read all safety information and never use the machine in any way that violates the manufacturer's instructions for safe use. The air fryer manual will provide details about your model's features and functions.

2. Cooking time: Many factors can affect cooking times, including volume, size, and temperature of the food, the thickness of breading, and so on. Even your local humidity levels can affect required cooking times. Wattage is another factor. A unit with a higher or lower wattage may cook somewhat faster or slower. For most recipes, total cooking time shouldn't vary by more than a minute or two. However, to avoid overcooking, check food early and often. Always start with the shortest cooking time listed in a recipe. Check for doneness at that point and continue cooking if necessary. When you try a recipe for the first time and the minimum cooking time is, say, 20 minutes or longer, check the dish after about 15 minutes just to be safe. If you are new to air frying, don't hesitate to pause your air fryer to open the drawer and check foods.

3. Minimum temperatures for food safety: Consuming undercooked fish, eggs, meats, game, poultry, seafood, or shellfish may increase your risk of foodborne illness. To ensure that foods are safe to eat, ground lamb, beef, pork, and veal should be cooked to a minimum of 160°F. All chicken and turkey should be cooked to a minimum of 165°F. Minimum safe temperatures for fish and seafood can vary.

4. Cooking in batches: Always cut foods into uniform pieces so they cook more evenly. Follow recipes to know whether foods can be stacked or if they must be cooked in a single layer. Directions will indicate whether you need to turn or shake the basket to redistribute foods during cooking. For foods that require longer cooking times, the first batch may cool quickly while the second batch is cooking. The solution is simple; air fryers do an excellent job of reheating foods. Right before your second batch finishes cooking, place your first batch on top so it reheats for serving. If there is not enough room in your air fryer basket, then wait until the second batch is done, remove it, and reheat the first batch for a minute or two. Also, you can buy a larger air fryer. Some models have a capacity of approximately 5 quarts.

5. Smoking: Select a suitable location for your unit. If possible, place it near your range so you can use the

vent hood if needed. Follow the manufacturer's instructions to protect your countertop and allow the required amount of open space around the back, sides, and top of your air fryer. Smoking isn't a frequent problem but does occur when cooking meats or other foods with a high-fat content. Adding water to the air fryer drawer can help sometimes. Coconut, for example, tends to smoke no matter what. Prevent this problem by keeping the drawer clean and free of food or fat buildup.

Air fryer tips

1. Use parchment paper for easy cleanup. Line the bottom of the air fryer basket or baking pan with parchment paper to catch excess grease.
2. Keep it clean. Keeping your air fryer clean will extend its life. After each use, wipe out the baking pan and the fryer basket with a slightly damp paper towel or cloth. If you cook meat or fish, soak your accessories in warm soapy water.
3. Drain excess fat. It will help to minimize smoke. Fatty foods such as chicken wings and steak can burn and create smoke that escapes from the air fryer. If this happens, pause the appliance and carefully drain the fat from the fryer basket or wipe off any oily grease from the food with a paper towel. Then resume cooking.

4. Preheat the air fryer before cooking. Preheating will ensure that the airflow and temperature are at their optimum levels when you place your food in the fryer, and your food will cook more evenly. This process takes 3 minutes or less.

5. Use a baking pan for breaded foods. Air circulation can cause bits of breading and small pieces of food to come loose and fly around the chamber. Cook foods inside the baking pan to prevent this problem.

6. Shake the basket. During the cooking process, pause the air fryer once or twice and gently shake the air fryer basket. This will redistribute the food, cooking it more evenly and allowing it to brown on all sides.

Function keys

- Play/Pause Button - The Play/Pause button allows you to pause during cooking to shake the air fryer basket or flip the food and ensure even cooking.

- Plus/Minus Button - This button is used to change the time or temperature.

- Keep Warm - This function keeps your food warm for 30 minutes.

- Food presets - This button gives you the ability to cook food without second-guessing. The time and temperature are already set, so new users find this to be a helpful option.

- Roast or Broil - You can roast or broil with this setting. When using a conventional oven, you need to brown the meat before roasting. You can skip this step when cooking with an air fryer.
- Dehydrate - This setting cooks and dries food at a low temperature for a few hours. You can create your favorite beef jerky or dried fruit with this option.

Features of your air fryer

1. Portable: The cooking device is portable and designed to be easily transferred from your kitchen storage cabinet to the countertop or another spot.
2. Automatic temperature control: You get perfectly cooked food every time with an air fryer.
3. Digital touch screen: You don't have to learn complicated cooking skills. Simplicity is built in with an air fryer. With a few taps on the touch screen, you can cook various foods easily.
4. Timer and buzzer: No need to worry about overcooking your food. The timer and buzzer will let you know when your food is fully cooked.

Air fryer vs. deep fryer

1. Oil usage: Air fryers use less oil; this means using an air fryer costs you less. You need to use a lot more oil

when deep-frying. Although you can reuse the oil, most health experts don't recommend it.

2. Healthy cooking: Fried foods such as air-fried French fries contain up to 80% less fat than most of the unhealthy, deep-fried options.

3. Cleaning: Compared to deep-frying, cleaning an air fryer is easy. You won't need to clean the deep fryer and the hard-to-spot oil vapor that settled on the kitchen walls and the countertop area.

4. Safety: An air fryer is safe to use. With a deep fryer, there is always a risk of accidents.

5. Multiple uses: You can only fry in a deep fryer. On the other hand, you can cook different types of foods in many different ways with an air fryer.

Air fryer vs. convection oven

1. Less hazard: An air fryer gives you a one-stop cooking solution. You often have to cook the food in a pan for a few minutes to get the color and bring out the aroma before you put it in the oven.

2. Safe: You can open and close the air fryer without the risk of burning yourself. With a traditional oven, there is always a risk of fire.

3. Speed: Food cooks faster in an air fryer.

4. Cleaning: Cleaning your air fryer is easy. On the other hand, cleaning an oven is time-consuming.

Air fryer vs. microwave

1. Cooking technique: An air fryer uses heat from a power source and a fan circulates the hot air evenly. On the other hand, a microwave uses high-frequency, short-length radio waves to produce heat.
2. Cooking time: A microwave takes less time to cook, but an air fryer produces more flavorful meals.
3. The health factor: An air fryer is considered healthier because you use less oil. Additionally, many people feel that the electromagnetic radiation of a microwave poses a health risk.

Air fryer vs. pressure cooker

1. Meals: With an air fryer, you can cook mostly crispy food. A pressure cooker helps you cook meals that require liquid.
2. Cooking method: An air fryer uses hot air to cook food. A pressure cooker uses hot liquid and steam to cook meals.
3. Heat and pressure usage: An air fryer always uses high heat to cook food. Pressure cookers use low, medium, and high-heat settings to cook food.
4. Healthier option: An air fryer is more beneficial than a pressure cooker. Pressure cooking can't make your food more nutritious, but an air fryer can.

Tips for the perfect air fry

1. Find a place for your air fryer: Find a place in your kitchen where it will always be easy to access the air fryer, to the point where you simply need to open the cooking container and add all your ingredients.

2. Temperature: Different recipes require different temperatures to ensure that the food is cooked correctly. Follow the recipe as precisely as possible to ensure that your food tastes delicious.

3. Aluminum foil: The aluminum foil helps with the cleaning and is often used to add even more gradual control to the cooking process for the ingredients.

4. Add a dash of water for fatty foods: You will notice a small drawer at the bottom of your air fryer where you can add a splash of water when you're cooking high-fat foods. If the fat becomes too hot and drips to the bottom for too long, it can sometimes start to smoke. Adding vegetables prevents smoke. But if you are only cooking meat, then it is good to add water to avoid the unpleasant smoke from rising.

5. Do not add too many ingredients: Do not overcrowd the air fryer's cooking basket. Ensure that the ingredients are all at one level, especially if you are preparing meat, to avoid uneven cooking.

6. Flip foods: Flip foods if you want both sides to have a

crispy coating. Flip your food halfway through the cooking time.

7. Mid-cook opening: Do not worry about opening the air fryer during the cooking process. Unlike other methods, the air fryer doesn't lose heat intensity if you open it in the middle of cooking. Once you close the top again, the device will go back to the correct temperature and cook the food.

8. The bottom basket: There is a basket at the bottom of the air fryer to collect grease. If you take out both the cooking basket and the bottom basket simultaneously and tip them over, the oil from the bottom will be transferred onto your plate along with food. Remove the bottom basket before removing the food.

9. Clean: Clean the air fryer after every use: Leftover food particles can grow mold, develop bacteria, and cause very unpleasant after-effects. So clean the air fryer after every use.

10. Drying: Once you clean the air fryer, reassemble the unit and the air fryer will dry itself within a few minutes.

Here are some of the cooking techniques that you can use with this appliance:

- Fry: You can avoid oil when cooking, but a little amount adds flavor and crunch to your food.

- Roast: You can produce high-quality roasted food in the air fryer
- Bake: You can bake bread, cookies, and pastries.
- Grill: It can effectively grill your food without a mess.

To start cooking, you just need to spray the fryer basket with some cooking spray, or put in a bit of cooking oil, then add the ingredients and adjust the temperature and time.

Mistakes when using an air fryer

1. You don't check your food enough: Air fryers have made it easy to pop food inside, set the time, and then leave it to cook away until the timer beeps. However, when cooking certain foods, you need to check them regularly to prevent overcooking. For example, foods like salmon have a fragile line between being cooked and overcooked.
2. You only cook fried foods: The air fryer is an incredibly versatile kitchen appliance. You can cook vegetables, meats, and even baked goods in it.
3. Overcrowding the basket: If you have too much food in at a time, the heat won't be distributed evenly. This can lead to a combination of burned and undercooked food in one basket.

BEST AND WORST FOODS TO AIR FRY

Best Foods for an Air Fryer	Worst Foods for an Air Fryer
French fries	Any food with a wet batter
Potatoes	Foods that require a lot of water, such as rice or pasta
Meat and poultry	Broccoli will dry out too much
Chickpeas for a crunchy snack	Olive oil may burn at the high heats
Air-fried donuts	Leafy greens won't cook evenly
Chicken nuggets	Salmon can overcook easily if you aren't carefully monitoring it
Small pizzas to create a crispy base	Cakes will dry out in an air fryer, if you are not careful
Crispy zucchini	Bacon will splash too much oil and make a mess in the air fryer
Frozen foods, including fried foods, frozen veggies, and frozen prepared meals	Too much cheese can cause a mess in the air fryer if it melts all over

Important safeguards

Warnings

- Do not place anything on top of the air fryer.
- Do not cover the air vents on the top, back, or side of the air fryer.
- Use oven mitts when removing foods from the air fryer.
- Do not leave the door open for an extended period.
- Always close the door gently.

Caution

- Plug the power cord into a 2-prong wall outlet.
- Do not use an extension cord with this product.

2

CHOOSING AN AIR FRYER

There are different types of air fryers available in the market. Below are a few things that you need to consider when buying one.

Price

- The price of air fryers ranges from $50 to $300.
- Higher-priced air fryers have a higher wattage and offer more cooking options. They also have preset programs.
- Lower-priced air fryers can be just as effective as the high priced ones.

Size

- 2-quart air fryers are suitable for 1 to 2 people.
- 3- to 4-quart air fryers are suited for a family of 3-to-4-persons.
- 5- to 8-quart air fryers work well for large families.
- A true convection air fryer oven is ideal for a bigger family.

DIFFERENT TYPES OF AIR FRYERS

Paddle-style

- You do not have to flip the food at the halfway mark with this type of air fryer. A paddle attached to the cooking basket moves the food and helps cook evenly. You can remove the paddle as needed to make various dishes.

Basket-type

- This model is most common. A perforated basket holds the food and cooks it evenly. You need to shake the food at least once during cooking.
- You can't make anything too soupy or saucy with this model.

Countertop convection oven

- It is not an air fryer, but cooks in a similar way
- They have a few settings that you can use to cook like an air fryer
- Have a large capacity
- Is more versatility
- Have multiple cooking options
- Take up more counter space
- Are more expensive

Combination air fryers

- Air fryer/pressure cooker combo or air fryer/toaster oven combo
- Can perform several cooking jobs

Buying guide for air fryers

What are the things you should consider before buying an air fryer?

- Capacity: Air fryers come in different sizes: small, medium, or large.
- Wattage: A standard air fryer usually uses 1500 watts. This, however, varies from one model to another. Before you go ahead and buy an air fryer, make sure your kitchen can support it.

- Temperature: The higher the temperature, the faster an air fryer will cook. This also means that the food won't absorb much oil while cooking batter-coated foods. You should only choose an air fryer that comes with proper temperature control. This will help you cook at the right temperature levels for various food items.

- Safety: You need to choose an air fryer that is well-insulated and comes with proper safety measures for when you pull out the tray. Look for air fryers that won't slip from the kitchen countertop. Automatic shut-off prevents overcooking.

Types of air fryers

There are basically two air types of fryers: convection oven air fryers and basket air fryers. The basket air fryers have a basket to hold the food.

1. Philips air fryer: This is a basket-type unit. This model has two versions, 2.75 quarts and 4 quarts. The Philips air fryer looks stylish and is the pioneer in air frying. However, the appliance is small compared to a oven-type air fryer, and the price is high.

2. GoWISE air fryer: This air fryer is cheaper than a Philips, and is available in three sizes: 2.75 quarts, 3.7 quarts, and 5.8 quarts. Users like the price of this air fryer but have issues with the nonstick coating.

3. Breville Smart Oven Air: This appliance is both a convection oven and an air fryer. It can roast, dehydrate, bake, and fry. This oven air fryer is 5.8 quarts and can bake a 13-inch pizza. Users like the multifunction ability of this appliance, however, they say that the price is high and it takes longer to preheat than a smaller air fryer.

4. Cuisinart AirFryer convection toaster oven: This appliance is cheaper than Breville. It can roast, warm, broil, bake, and air fry. Users like this oven, but have problems with the durability of the knobs and have trouble controlling the temperature.

5. T-Fal Actifry air fryer: This appliance comes with a unique, built-in paddle that flips the food during cooking, so you don't have to open the appliance and do it manually. This air fryer holds 2.75 quarts; it is good for cooking fries, but not so good for breaded or larger foods. The other problem is that there is no temperature control.

6. Black+Decker PuriFry air fryer: This appliance is affordable and has basic air frying functionality. The size of this air fryer is 2 quarts. Users like this air fryer because it is affordable, but the letters are too small on the dials, so it is difficult to read.

7. Cosori air fryer: This air fryer is affordable, has a unique design, and large capacity. It comes in two

sizes, 3.7 quarts and 5.8 quarts. Users love the price and the sleek design of this air fryer.

8. Instant Pot Vortex Plus air fryer: This air fryer has two versions, 6 quarts and 10 quarts. This appliance can air fry, dehydrate, broil, roast, toast, and bake. Its large capacity means you can cook for the whole family.

9. Ninja Air Fryer Max XL: This is a 5.5-quart basket-style air fryer that cooks fries and chicken wings well. The appliance comes with a broiling rack. The settings are accessible and it is easy to control the temperature to achieve different cooking results.

10. Chefman TurboFry: This 3.7-quart air fryer produces crispy, even air frying. You need to empty the grease between cooking each batch.

11. Power XL Air Fryer Pro: This air fryer oven gives you more space to cook with multiple racks included. The downside is that you have to rotate the racks for more even cooking.

12. Cosori Air Fryer: This air fryer has a 3.7-quart capacity and offers a lot of cooking space. The appliance can make crispy fries and wings.

13. GoWISE USA 7-Quart Electric Air Fryer: If you want to cook large batches of food, this is the appliance you want. The air fryer offers three additional racks which allows you to cook up to four layers of food simultaneously.

14. Dash Compact Air Fryer: This air fryer has a 1.7 quart

capacity and is ideal for one person. You can use the 400°F maximum temperature to air fry most foods.

15. Gourmia 6-Quart Air Fryer: This unit has a square cooking chamber and makes it easy to create different layers to cook several foods at once. You can cook veggies, protein, and carbs – all at once.

16. Ninja Foodi 8-in-1 Toaster Oven and Air Fryer: This appliance is everything in one unit. It can toast, bake, grill, and do other cooking jobs. Even though the appliance is big, it fits nicely in a small apartment.

17. Chefman 6.3-Quart Air Fryer: This air fryer comes with two racks and makes it easy to cook different types of foods at once. A see-through glass door means you can see what you are cooking.

18. Avalon Bay Air Fryer: If you are looking for a non-digital air fryer, then this is it. It doesn't have a digital display, and some users find it useful.

19. Bella 2.6-Quart Air Convection Fryer: If you are looking for an air fryer for a one- or two-person household, then this is the one. It is easy to use and durable.

Let's discuss them in detail.

PHILIPS TWIN TURBOSTAR AIRFRYER XXL

Philips is the pioneer in air fryer appliances. It introduced the first air fryer in 2010 at an electronics fair in Berlin. We will discuss the Philips Twin TurboStar XXL.

The Twin TurboStar XXL is 12 inches tall, 17 inches deep, and 12 inches tall. Currently, it is on sale on Amazon for $250.

Spaces

The appliance has a temperature range of 175° to 400°F. The dial allows you to set the time in intervals (between 1 and 60 minutes). You can choose different settings for different foods, including fish, steak, chicken, defrost, and cake. The LCD shows the time and temperature during the cooking process. The air fryer has a 1-year limited warranty. There is a free recipe book available with this model.

Setup process

Open the package and wash the pan and basket with soap and water. Preheat the air fryer for a few minutes before cooking.

Positives

The capacity of this air fryer is 4 quarts, or 3 pounds of food. When cooking, the air fryer should stay cool to the touch everywhere except the back. If the air fryer discharges a lot of heat, it is not operating efficiently. The pan, fat reducer tray, and basket are all dishwasher-safe.

Cons to consider

You need to use an oil sprayer when cooking foods. You can't add too much oil.

PHILIPS PREMIUM COLLECTION AIRFRYER XXL

The Philips Airfryer XXL has a hefty load capacity. It is not as large as an oven, but can handle big cooking needs. You can cook up to 3 pounds of frozen snacks, French fries, or potatoes in it. You can even cook a whole chicken in it. Currently, the price is $559 on Amazon. The Airfryer XXL is powerful with a 1,725-watt heating system.

The price is the first drawback of this air fryer. The confusing temperature control is another drawback of this appliance. The air fryer parts are dishwasher-safe, but you have more pieces to wash.

Confusing controls

The temperature control is a bit difficult and confusing. Also, the indicator light is useless.

GOWISE AIR FRYER

The GoWise air fryer has a touchscreen, eight preset functions to cook a wide variety of food, and a large capacity of 7-quarts.

The air fryer can reheat, bake, grill, dehydrate, broil, roast, fry, and keep warm. The temperature ranges from 180° to 400°F. It comes with a PFOA-free coated basket, three stackable racks, and a crisper tray for easy cleanup. If you have a big family, then this is the fryer for you.

The downsides

It doesn't have a removable basket like other models. Some users say that the control panel of this air fryer could be a bit more intuitive.

CUISINART AIRFRYER CONVECTION TOASTER OVEN

This Cuisinart AirFryer toaster oven is a multicooker with a $250 price tag and comes with several distinctive cooking features: a baking/drip pan, a rack, and an air fryer basket. This air fryer oven can do several cooking jobs well. For example, it can toast bread beautifully. It can cook vegetables, snacks, nuggets, wings, and fries with ease. The baking feature of this device offers both low and high fan speed convection cooking, and the temperature range is 200° to 450°F. The appliance can also roast, broil, and dehydrate. If you want the features of both an air fryer and oven in one appliance, then this device is for you.

T-FAL ACTIFRY AIR FRYER

This air fryer does more than other basic air fryers. The appliance is equipped with a motorized stirring arm and can mix food during cooking. Therefore, it can cook a wide variety of dishes including risotto, and fried rice. However, the paddle can be rough on soft foods like fish fillets and hamburger patties. The appliance can't handle too much liquid.

This Actifry model has basic controls and makes cooking simple. If you want crispy air-fried food that is uniformly golden brown and delicious, then this is the air fryer for you.

BLACK+DECKER PURIFRY AIR FRYER

This air fryer is affordable, compact, and simple to operate. It makes air-fried foods that taste delicious. The downside is that it is small, so you can't cook meals for a big family. The air fryer doesn't have a motorized stirring arm, so you need to open the air fryer at the halfway mark and stir the food.

The appliance is small, so it shouldn't take much of your counter space. The air fryer has only two dials on its front side: one dial controlling the cooking time and another for temperature. The problem is that the text is tiny and difficult to read. This air fryer is ideal for a small family.

COSORI 5.7-QUART AIR FRYER

The Cosori 5.7-quart air fryer is an efficient cooking appliance. It has 11 presets and preheat settings. This cooking device is one of the largest options on the market and is bulky.

Features

- 5.8-quart, nonstick basket
- Digital interface
- Preheat function
- 120V and 1700W
- Shake reminder
- Keep warm and auto-shutoff function
- 2 year warranty

The Cosori presets include:

- Steak
- Chicken
- Seafood
- Shrimp
- Bacon
- Frozen foods
- French fries
- Vegetables
- Root vegetables
- Bread

- Desserts

Cooking-related notes

During cooking, air comes out of the back, so there is some noise, but it isn't terribly loud. You need to use an oil mister to grease the food.

Pros

- Faster cooking times
- Dishwasher-safe

Cons

- It takes up a lot of room on the counter
- Preset cooking time may not work. You need to follow the trial-and-error method to know the exact cooking time

COSORI SMART AIR FRYER

Cosori has a smart version available. It offers various smart options, including:

- You can use your phone to schedule, monitor, and adjust cooking times
- You can set up cooking times in advance

- Alexa-enabled, so you can use Amazon Echo devices

INSTANT POT VORTEX PLUS

The instant brand is already famous with its Instant Pots. Now it is introducing air fryers. This appliance is more than just an air fryer. It can dehydrate, broil, bake, roast, and rotate for rotisserie-style recipes.

Design

This device looks good with its compact design. It has a touchscreen panel on top and a stainless-steel front. All the accessories, including rotisserie spit parts, trays, and baskets, are dishwasher-safe. The design drawbacks are that the display shows the unit as being ON during preheating, instead of showing PRE. Also, the 400°F temperature is a bit limiting. A few frozen foods recommend that you heat your oven to 425°F. Also, several countertop ovens heat up to 500°F.

Cooking modes

It has seven options: rotate, dehydrate, air fry, reheat, roast, broil, and bake. This appliance does more than air frying, and is in direct competition with other toaster ovens. The dehydrator is one of the most interesting features of the Vortex Plus. You can make your own apple or banana chips or beef jerky with it.

Roast and rotate modes

You can use this feature to turn the air fryer basket or rotate the rotisserie spit. Usually, you can cook a 4-pound whole chicken. However, if you use the baking tray, you can cook larger chickens.

NINJA AIR FRYER MAX XL

Top features of this air fryer

- 5.5-quart capacity
- Cooks at 450°F
- Ceramic-coated nonstick basket
- Multiple functions
- 1,550 watts
- Seven manual programs included
- Advanced control panel

The Ninja air fryer is an air fryer that can finish any cooking tasks within minutes. The ceramic-coated basket is an added advantage of this air fryer. You can use this appliance for dehydrating, roasting, reheating, and air frying. The Ninja air fryer is the perfect machine for making casseroles, chickens, fries, and fried veggies. It has a one-touch control panel to help you set up the fryer.

The air fryer has a large basket that holds 5.5 quarts. You can easily fit a 3 ½-pound chicken in it.

Important tips to remember:

- Preheat the basket for three minutes
- Shake the food at the halfway point

Pros

- Generous capacity
- Handy presets to make cooking easier for you
- Dishwasher-safe

Cons

- Larger worktop footprint
- No power cable storage
- Heavier than most air fryers

CHEFMAN TURBOFRY

This air fryer is compact, lightweight, and doesn't take up too much counter space.

Digital controls

There are five touch buttons: a start/stop button, one for time, and another for temperature. Two others are plus and minus buttons. The temperature ranges from 200° to 400°F. The cooking basket has a 14.7-cup or 3.5-liter capacity. This air fryer is perfect for two- to three-person families.

You can bake salmon burgers or French fries, and roast vegetables in it. There are no cooking presets on this machine. You need to read the manual to know the recommended cooking times. You need to flip the food manually during the halfway mark.

The digital version of Chefman TurboFry costs $80. There is an analog version that costs $60.

Pros

- Affordable
- Less noise
- Easy to clean
- Intuitive controls
- Space-saving design

Cons

- Temperature is fixed at 400°F
- Inserting the cooking basket can be a bit tricky

Note

There are rubber caps that are attached to the inner basket. These can get loose and get mixed with your food. So you need to be careful about this.

POWER XL AIR FRYER PRO

This air fryer is available in 6-quart and 8-quart sizes. If you buy the 8-quart air fryer, you will not need a deep fryer, toaster oven, or microwave. In the box, you will receive:

- 3 recipe books
- Rotisserie stand
- Rotating Mesh Basket
- Drip tray
- 10 rotisserie skewers

This appliance has eight presets and can reach up to 400°F. It has a viewing screen at the front so you can watch while the air fryer cooks your food.

Spacious

You can cook a rotisserie chicken or an entire duck in this air fryer.

Pros

- The size: This is a big air fryer. The removable racks mean you get more space.
- The price: The air fryer is a bit costly, but if you want to bake, air fry, and spit-roast large quantities of food regularly, then you need this appliance.

Cons

- The two-month warranty: Other air fryers have warranties of six months to one year.
- The user manual: The user manual is not very thorough.
- Large machine: It will take more counter space.

GOWISE USA 7-QUART ELECTRIC AIR FRYER

This air fryer has a 1,700-watt power motor and a 7-quart extra-large capacity. It has 3 stackable racks, a digital touch display, and offers a dehydrator function. The digital display offers 8 functions.

The air fryer's large capacity allows you to cook for your whole family. The eight cooking functions include air fry, warm, reheat, dehydrate, broil, roast, bake, and grill. The temperature ranges from 180° to 400°F and the timer goes up to 60 minutes.

Pros

- Large capacity
- LED digital touch screen
- Up to 24 hours cooking time
- 3 stackable racks
- Dehydration function

Cons

- Cramped interface
- Display not easy to read

Features

- Large cooking space to easily cook a whole chicken or 4 to 5 burgers
- Large control panel
- Cooking timer
- 8 cooking functions
- Easy cleanup of the removable parts
- FDA compliant
- 1-year warranty
- Recipe book with 100 recipes

This air fryer is perfect for a big family, and the price is also reasonable.

DASH COMPACT AIR FRYER

Pros

- Small footprint
- The exterior of the unit doesn't heat up during cooking
- Auto shutoff feature

Cons

- Small 1.6-quart capacity
- Only 1,000 watts of power
- Will cook food unevenly if you are not careful

Design

This air fryer is compact and lightweight. The appliance has only a 1.6-quart fry basket, which is ideal for a small family. There is a manual knob placed at the front of the air fryer. You can use it to set the cooking time. Two indicator lights below the temperature knob show you if it is on. The air fryer doesn't have any pre-programmed options (such as fish, meat, or French fries). You need to use the trial-and-error method to find the most effective cooking methods with this appliance.

Users who have used it to make French fries and apple chips say that they cooked unevenly. So you have to decide if you want to purchase this air fryer or not.

GOURMIA 6-QUART AIR FRYER

This air fryer is an attractive appliance with little to no issues.

Pros

- Dishwasher-safe
- Attractive appliance
- 8 presets
- Impressive LED display
- Inexpensive
- Easy to use
- Lightweight
- Touchscreen digital control
- Adjustable 60-minute timer
- Includes: nonstick basket with 2 removable crisping trays

Cons

- Cylindrical design
- You may find several presets not useful
- Need a lot of room

Looks

This is a good-looking appliance with a cylindrical body. The touchscreen LCD display adds value, and the capacity is 6 quarts. The air fryer comes with options for customization of temperature and time and has eight presets:

- Chicken
- Steak
- Bacon
- Fish
- French fries
- Shrimp
- Pizza
- Bake

How to use

- Place the inner basket in the appliance
- Add food to the air fryer basket
- Choose your preferred time and temperature
- Flip the food halfway through
- Finish cooking and enjoy

Buy this appliance

- If you are on a budget
- If you like to enjoy a lot of the same things

NINJA FOODI 8-IN-1 TOASTER OVEN AND AIR FRYER

The Ninja brand is renowned for its Instant Pot appliance. Now it is introducing a new product – an air fryer oven. It has the features of a convection oven, dehydrator, and toaster oven. The appliance has a one-year limited warranty.

This appliance has 8-in-1 functionality:

- Air fryer
- Toast
- Air roast
- Air broil
- Bake
- Dehydrate
- Bagel
- Keep warm

Features

- 8-in-1 functionality
- 1,800 watt
- Cooks up to 60% faster than a traditional oven
- Stainless steel construction
- XL capacity

Pros

- Multifunctional
- Cooks evenly
- Easy cleaning
- Preheats almost instantly
- Flip capabilities
- Quiet operation
- Easy control panel
- Versatile
- It doesn't heat up the kitchen

Cons

- Unable to cook a whole chicken
- The anti-stick pan may warp at 400°F
- Quantity is only enough for 3 to 4 people
- A bit expensive

Design

The appliance is designed efficiently, so it takes up less space on the countertop. The stainless-steel body makes it durable. It can cook six chicken breasts or nine slices of toast.

Control panel

Using the digital control panel is easy. There is a knob to set the timer and temperature.

Performance

The oven preheats automatically within just 1 minute. It is quieter than most air fryers and comes with an easy-to-understand owner's guide. 1,800 wattage enables faster cooking. It can cook chicken breasts within 20 minutes. The appliance is large enough to cook nine slices of toast, or six chicken breasts, or a 12-inch frozen pizza. This appliance is a fair air fryer and an excellent toaster.

Cleaning

The accessories are easy to clean. The inside of the oven appliance is accessible enough to wipe down any leftover mess post-cooking.

CHEFMAN 6.3 QUART AIR FRYER

This air fryer stands out because of its sleek design, large capacity, convenient features, and numerous functionalities. This versatile device serves as an oven, food dehydrator, rotisserie, and air fryer. You can cook chicken, pies, pizzas, and other things in this appliance.

Features

The air fryer has a sleek design. It has a large see-through window at the front and a two-tiered rack. The LCD has eight presets that include the rotating setting as well as interior light, time, and temperature.

The air fryer comes with all the necessary accessories, including a rotating basket, a retrieval tool, a drip tray, rotisserie spits, and airflow racks.

Pros

- 8 touchscreen presets
- Made of BPA-free plastic
- Multifunctional
- Accessories
- Large 6-liter capacity
- 1-year warranty
- Dishwasher-safe
- Advanced safety technology

Cons

- Price is high
- Users find a 10-degree temperature control increment difficult; a 5-degree increment was preferred

AVALON BAY AIR FRYER

Top features of this air fryer

- It gives you several cooking options like roasting, baking, and grilling
- It comes with a recipe book
- Built-in timer
- Temperature control
- 1-year warranty
- Durable 2-piece baking set

Pros

- Compact design with a unique feature
- Non-slip feet
- 30-minute timer
- Less expensive

Cons

- Suitable for a small family. If you have a large family, then you have to cook in batches.
- Cooking an entire dish is complicated
- It takes up a lot of room on the counter

You can cook a small, whole chicken in it. If you want to cook anything with runny batter, freeze the food first for better results. You can purchase a cake kit separately and bake a cake in it.

Easy to clean

The air fryer is easy to clean, and the removable parts are dishwasher-safe.

Verdict

Ideal for individuals, small families, or couples.

BELLA 2.6 QUART AIR CONVECTION OVEN

This is an air fryer convection oven combination. This appliance is one of the most popular air fryers on the market. The air fryer allows you to cook a variety of dishes with ease. You can cook over 2 pounds of food in this appliance.

Pros

- Easy to use
- Good value for money
- 2-year warranty
- 1,500 watt
- Convection circulating system
- Temperature up to 400°F
- Dishwasher-safe

- Includes nonstick pan and frying basket

Cons

- No digital display
- Too small for a big family

Minimal controls

The controls are simple and easy to understand. You just turn the dial to the desired setting and you are done.

EMERIL LAGASSE POWER AIR FRYER 360

Pros

- 12 versatile cooking presets
- Bright interior light
- Easy LCD control panel

Cons

- Takes up more counterspace
- Noisy
- Tricky to clean

With 12 preset cooking functions, the appliance can reheat, roast, toast, bake, dehydrate, fry, among other things.

Setting up this appliance is easy. Remove the appliance from the packaging. Then plug it in. Insert the accessories and preheat for 10 minutes when using them for the first time.

Design

Some might find it too large for their kitchen.

Features

The air fryer uses 360° Quick Cook technology. Five heating elements are placed in the top and bottom parts of the appliance. Twelve preset cooking functions include warm, dehydrate, reheat, slow cook, rotisserie, broil, roast, bake, pizza, bagel, toast, and fry. The air fryer comes with a rotisserie spit, pizza rack, baking pan, and a crisper tray.

Performance

The appliance is powerful but noisy.

BEST-SELLING AIR FRYERS

ULTREAN AIR FRYER 4.2 QUART

The price of this air fryer is $69.99. It has 1,500 watts of power with a 1-year warranty.

Features

- Aside from frying, you can also bake, grill, and roast

your favorite foods.

- Comes with an adjustable temperature setting (180° to 400°F) and an auto switch off timer (1 to 30 minutes).
- A dishwasher-safe basket, heat-resistant handle, and nonstick pan make it easier to cook and clean.
- It has an LCD display and comes with a recipe book.

COSORI SMART WIFI AIR FRYER

This appliance is a smart air fryer priced at $119. It works with Alexa and Google assistant.

Features

- The first air fryer you can control and monitor with your mobile device.
- Control the air fryer with app and voice commands.
- The air fryer has a smaller footprint and saves you space on your countertop.
- Has 11 built-in one-touch presets (including preheat, desserts, bread, root vegetables, vegetables, French fries, frozen foods, bacon, shrimp, seafood, poultry, and steak)

TAOTRONICS 6-QUART AIR FRYER

The air fryer is priced at $101.99. It has 1,750 watts of power and a 360° air convection system

Features

- The air fryer has 11 preset menus with adjustable time and temperature settings.
- 6-quart cooking basket means you can cook family-sized meals easily.
- It follows FDA safety regulations and has overheating protection and automatic shutoff.
- Ergonomic 13° inclined digital display panel ensures easy operation.

NUWAVE BRIO 6-QUART AIR FRYER

This is a digital air fryer with six easy presets.

Features

- This air fryer has a preheat and reheat function. It has a basket divider, precise temperature control, and a recipe book included.
- The temperature ranges from 100° to 400°F. You can roast, grill, broil, air fry, and dehydrate your food. The basket divider makes it possible for you to cook two things simultaneously.

10-IN-1 AIR FRYER OVEN, 20-QUART AIR FRYER TOASTER OVEN COMBO

This 1,800 watt large air fryer has plenty of cooking space.

- This air fryer oven offers a 20-quart unit that allows you to make meals for a big family.
- It allows you to dehydrate, rotisserie, toast, roast, grill, bake, and air fry.
- Ten preset options make it easier to cook.
- It comes with 13 accessories, including a removable drip tray, a pair of oven mitts, five dehydrating racks, a chicken fork, fetch rack, drip tray, roasting basket, fry net basket, and a skewer rotisserie.

KALORIK 26-QUART DIGITAL MAXX AIR FRYER OVEN

This 26-quart air fryer oven has quite a few benefits due to its large capacity.

Features

- This air fryer oven offers the functionality of 10 different appliances in one unit. It has a digital LED display with 21 presets.
- The appliance runs on a turbo Maxx airflow system,

which cooks food 50% faster than standard ovens and 30% faster than the other air fryer ovens.

- This air fryer can toast nine slices of bread, bake a 12-inch pizza, or roast a whole chicken.

- Accessories include steak tray, rotisserie spit, rotisserie handle, rack handle, crumb tray, baking pan, bacon tray, air rack, and air fryer basket.

- The Kalorik brand has 90 years of experience in manufacturing cooking appliances.

- ETL-certified and has a 1-year warranty.

INNSKY AIR FRYER, 10.6-QUART AIR OVEN

This air fryer oven has 1500 watts of power.

Features

- This appliance is not only an air fryer, but also an oven toaster, pizza grill, dehydrator, and rotisserie. Temperature ranges from 150° to 400°F.

- The extra-large capacity allows you to prepare family-sized meals. You can easily cook authentic kebabs, turkey breast, pork roast, and chicken wings.

- Digital display allows you to touch and change the settings instead of manually guessing.

- It comes with six extra accessories: eight skewers, two mesh racks, one rotisserie basket, one removal tool, one rotisserie shaft, and one drip tray.

COMFEE 3.7-QUART ELECTRIC AIR FRYER

This air fryer has a stainless-steel finish.

Features

- This air fryer is multifunction with eight selectable menus. The menus are fish, shrimp, meat, chicken legs, chicken wings, French fries, defrost, and cake.
- Rapid air circulation technology is used in this appliance to make your healthier dishes faster.
- Overheat protection and auto-shutoff.
- UL-Certified, BPA- and PFOA-free
- 1-year manufacturer warranty

UTEN AIR FRYER XL

This 5.8-quart air fryer has 1,700 watts of power.

Features

- 5.8-quart capacity means you can cook a regular size chicken. This air fryer is ideal for a family with 2 to 8 members.
- Auto shutoff feature prevents your food from being overcooked.

INSTANT POT OMNI PLUS

This is an 11-in-1 toaster oven air fryer.

Features

- Large capacity allows you to roast a whole chicken, bake a 12-inch pizza, or make a cake.
- It is a multifunction toaster oven and air fryer with 11 presets. You can reheat, proof, slow cook, broil, bake, roast, toast, dehydrate, and air fry with this appliance.
- It comes with a set of accessories: a rotisserie lift, rotisseries spits, forks, an air fryer basket, a cooking pan, and an oven rack.

GREEK CHEF AIR FRYER TOASTER OVEN

The Greek Chef multi cooker air fryer functions as a countertop oven and a convection air fryer.

Features

- This air fryer is family size and designed to save space. It has a capacity of 24 quarts with three rack levels. You can prepare meals for up to 10 people with this appliance.
- A 1,700-watt motor helps to cook food in a healthy way.

- The appliance has seven modes: keep warm, French fries, vegetables, skewer, defrost, cookies, wings, toast, steak, pizza, fish, chicken, and smart cake.
- It comes with four extra accessories: a drip tray, oven rack, air fryer basket, and baking pan.

OMMO AIR FRYER OVEN

This is a 1,800 watt, 17-quart air fryer toaster oven

Features

- This is an all-in-one air fryer oven. You can use it as an oven, toaster, pizza grill, dehydrator, rotisserie, and air fryer. The temperature ranges from 90° to 400°F. The 17-quart capacity allows you to prepare family-sized meals.
- The air fryer is simple to operate, and the eight preset cooking menu makes cooking even easier. The automatic shutoff feature prevents overcooking and overheating. See-through front door lets you see the progress of the food while it is cooking.
- It comes with extra accessories: one removal tool, one rotisserie shaft, one drip tray, one rotisserie basket, eight skewers, and two wire racks.
- Made with food-grade material and includes a 1-year warranty.

ULTREAN 8.5 QUART AIR FRYER

This is a versatile, 7-in-1 cooking appliance

Features

- This is an all-in-one multifunctional cooker that can bake, grill, roast, and fry all your favorite meals.
- A large cooking capacity lets you cook for 6 to 8 persons with ease.
- Seven cooking presets means you can do more with this appliance
- 1-year warranty

MOOSOO 10-IN-1 AIR FRYER TOASTER OVEN

This is an air fryer toaster oven with a variety of features.

Features

- This air fryer toaster oven includes 10 versatile presets: defrost, cookies, broil, bake, roast, pizza, dehydrate, rotisserie, toast, air fry, and also has two fan speeds.
- Six accessories kits include: removable crumb tray, fetch rack, rotisserie spit, baking pan, wire rack, and air fryer basket.
- Large 24-quart capacity, so you can cook for the whole family. You can fry 1 kg of French fries, roast a whole

4-pound chicken, bake a 12-inch pizza, or toast six pieces of bread.

- The appliance has intuitive digital and convenient dial controls, and a large LED screen. Unlike other machines, it offers a wide temperature range from 150° to 450°F. Timer ranges from 1 minute to 60 minutes.
- The appliance has a stainless-steel body. It is durable and easy to clean.
- Two high-speed fans make sure you get healthy meals quickly.

NEW HOUSE KITCHEN DIGITAL 6.8-QUART AIR FRYER

This is a digital air fryer with a large capacity.

Features

- Adjustable temperature setting. You can set the temperature from 175° to 400°F to cook various foods.
- If you want to bake pizzas, reheat leftover foods, and air fry vegetables or frozen foods, this machine is for you.
- This air fryer has a 6.8-quart capacity and can cook for your whole family.
- 1-year warranty

CROWNFUL 10-IN-1 AIR FRYER TOASTER OVEN

This is an air fryer toaster oven.

Features

- This multifunctional air fryer oven grills, toasts, reheats, dehydrates, cooks, roasts, fries, and bakes.
- A digital touch screen makes it easier to cook.
- The 360° hot air circulation technology offers you healthier food.
- It comes with additional accessories, including one rotisserie shaft, one drip tray, two mesh racks, two removal tools, and one rotisserie basket.
- 10.6-quart capacity means it is perfect for making large batches of food for your family and it comes with a recipe book.

SBOLY 8 MODE AIR FRYER

This is an air fryer with a digital touch screen and 6.3-quart capacity.

Features

- This air fryer has an LCD touch screen for easier and faster cooking. Eight preset modes make cooking easier for beginner users. You can cook fish, shrimp, steak, chicken, mixed vegetables, pizza, cake, and French fries in this air fryer.

- Wide temperature range from 180° to 400°F.
- The internal part of this air fryer is coated with nonstick water-based paint that provides better protection. This ensures that your food is residue-free.
- Large cooking area. Enables you to serve 3 to 6 people at a time.

BEST CHOICE PRODUCTS 16.9-QUART AIR FRYER

This is a huge 16.8-quart, 1,800 watt, 10-in-1 air fryer countertop oven.

Features

- Extra-large capacity. The appliance offers enough space to cook a whole turkey, chicken, and other family-sized meals. The see-through front panel enables you to see the cooking process without letting heat out.
- All-in-one appliance with ten presets. You can view the presets on the LCD touchscreen display. Twelve accessories include a rotating basket, a skewer rack set, and wire racks.

- Made with FDA-grade material that helps to avoid unwanted aftertastes.
- 1,800-watt motor helps to cook food in the healthiest way possible.

BIG BOSS OIL-LESS AIR FRYER

Made mostly with glass, this is one innovative air frying machine.

Features

- Enjoy your favorite foods without extra oil or calories. Bake, grill, fry, or roast with little to no oil.
- Simple and easy operation with two dials: timer with auto-shutoff and temperature control.
- The glass bowl design allows you to see your food cooking without interfering.
- Up to 16-quart capacity is large enough to cook a full turkey.
- You can cook two different foods with two different cooking requirements.
- 1,300 watts of power with triple cooking power: convection, halogen, and infrared heat.
- No need to preheat because of the instant heat technology. You do not have to thaw frozen foods before cooking them.
- 2-year warranty

Accessories

- Grill pan: This pan is needed for grilling and searing fish, meat, and vegetables in your air fryer. Before buying, make sure that your air fryer supports a grill pan.
- Air fryer liners: They make cleaning easier.
- Air fryer rack: It allows you to cook different foods in your air fryer.
- Baking pans: You can use these to bake cakes, bread, pizza, and more.
- Oil sprayer: Nonstick cooking spray can damage the basket surface, so use an oil sprayer instead.
- Heat-resistant tongs: You need them to shift food during cooking.
- Silicone cups: Good for cupcakes and egg cups.

You can also buy a full accessory pack for your air fryer:

- Oil brush
- Tongs
- Silicone cupcake mold
- Disposable paper liners
- Silicone mat
- Pizza pan
- Baking pan
- Two cooking racks

SETTING UP YOUR AIR FRYER

To choose the finest air fryer, remember these tips:

1. Cost: The price is the first criteria, but it should not be the only one. Bear in mind that a little higher investment can give good results in the long run.
2. Warranty: Who will respond if any problems occur? Having a reliable technical service is always an advantage.
3. Capacity: How many people do you usually cook for daily? Think about whether you purchase anything huge or small for your everyday meals.
4. Dimensions (required space in the kitchen): Where will you place your new air fryer? There is usually ample space in the kitchen. Think about where you are going to keep it before choosing it.

5. Replacement parts: Are replacement parts easily available? Always pick the appliances that can be restored to extend their life.

6. Consumption: Keep in mind that the power will be transferred directly to your electricity bill. Choose properly.

7. Previous users' opinions: A must in any current purchase decision is to know the experiences of prior users and their evaluation of actual use.

What should you bear in mind before purchasing an air fryer?

1. Type of frying basket: Baskets that can be separated to wash thoroughly are preferable. The material is also important. The metallic ones allocate the heat more rapidly. On the other hand, the ceramic ones are easier to clean. Several models merge the best of two worlds and offer metallic baskets with nonstick veneers.

2. Capacity: What you choose will depend mostly on the size and quantity of food you need to make in a single cycle of your fryer. It is, in general, not necessary to have a large machine, but if your family is huge or you usually cook for numerous days at a time, you should choose one of the models with a higher capacity. Some can even roast a whole chicken.

3. Preset programs: Many air fryers have presets for some of the most common foods, such as roast, roast

chicken, steaks, chops, pie, and much more. They are very convenient since, with a click of a button, you are able to cook food at the right temperature. Several models even allow you to create custom programs and keep them in memory.

4. Programmable timer/start: This model is worth choosing because it lets you schedule the precise time at which the food begins cooking so that it is freshly made right at the moment you are going to sit at the table. In many instances, you can leave everything arranged inside the fryer and go out to do your work knowing that it will begin cooking at the precise time to ensure that the meal is ready on time.

5. Preheating time: Some older fryers needed to preheat for up to 10 minutes before they could cook your food sufficiently, making you waste your time and consuming more energy than necessary. Newer models begin to heat almost right away.

The setup

First, open the packaging and read the enclosed manual. It is highly important that you read the manual before using the fryer. Here are steps you should take:

Placement

- Place the air fryer on a wooden cutting board or a heat-safe surface. During cooking, the bottom part of the air fryer gets hot.
- Usually, there is a heat exhaust at the back of the air fryer, so make sure there is at least 5 inches of space between the air fryer and the wall.
- Do not place anything on top of the machine.

Initial setup

- Read the manual first. Each model and brand are a bit different.
- Clean the air fryer accessories with hot soapy water, then use a dish towel to dry them.
- Assemble the air fryer and then preheat the air fryer for a few minutes to remove the factory oils and smells.

To remove the new air fryer smell

- In an oven-safe bowl, pour 1 cup white vinegar. Add 1 tbsp. of lemon juice and place the bowl into the air fryer basket.
- Run the air fryer at 400°F for 5 to 10 minutes.
- Repeat if you can still smell the odor.

Tips for first-time users

- You will hear a loud noise when the air fryer is running.
- You need to shake the basket several times for even cooking.
- It will cook faster if you put less food in the basket. If you put too much food in, it will take more time.
- To prevent your food from getting too dark too quickly, cook your food at a slightly lower temperature. This will help to prevent overcooking your food. You can use a lower temperature (25°F less) to prevent burning.

Using the controls

- Play/Pause button: You can start cooking with this setting and pause to shake the food basket.
- Plus/Minus button: You adjust time and temperature with this setting.
- Keep warm: You can keep food warm once the cooking is finish with this setting.

Food presets

- Most of the air fryers have food presets (such as keep

warm, fries/chips, chicken, steak, shrimp, pork, cake, and fish)

Safety precautions:

- You have to place your air fryer in an open space.
- If you must place your air fryer in a tight kitchen space, make sure there are no cabinets or cupboards above.
- Placing your air fryer in an open space will prevent overheating.
- Ideally, you should use oven mitts to avoid burning your hands, but if you do not have any, you should use something else to remove the air fryer basket from the air fryer.

Handling your food

- Allow your foods to cool before tasting them.
- Avoid overconsuming breaded and coated foods. Ideally, you should eat them only once or twice a week.

BPA-free air fryer

- Make sure your air fryer is BPA-free. You can find this information on the product website or in the product specifications.

- Stay close to your air fryer when it is running. Do not allow children to use it when you are not at home.

Air fryer tips for beginners

1. The right size air fryer: You need to buy an air fryer that is the right size for your family. If you are a family of two, then a 3.7-quart or smaller is enough. You need a bigger (5.8 quarts or above) air fryer for a family of 3 or more.

2. Clean: Before using the air fryer, you should clean all of the parts. Use a mild detergent and soft cloth to wash the accessories. Then wipe dry.

3. Give the appliance some space: While cooking, the air fryer can warm up to 400°F, so make sure there is at least 5 inches of space all around the air fryer.

4. Grease your basket: Use oil misters to grease the bottom of the air fryer. This will prevent food from getting stuck on the bottom, and food will get the golden-brown color you want.

5. Avoid aerosol sprays: Avoid aerosol sprays because they can damage your air fryer basket.

6. Heating: Do not use the highest setting when setting the temperature. Cooking at a lower temperature will help you to prevent your food from becoming hard, dry, and chewy.

7. Don't overcrowd the basket: Overcrowding your air fryer basket will result in uneven cooking.

8. Use a toothpick: Often, the hot air can shift food items to a corner, so use a utensil or a toothpick to hold the top item down. This works with items such as grilled cheese sandwiches.

9. Preheating: Some recipes require that you preheat your air fryer for 2 to 3 minutes.

10. Use presets: If you are a beginner cook, then presets are great for you. Presets will make sure that you get the right time and temperature.

11. Find recipes: Check out Pinterest or cookbooks for air fryer recipes.

12. Shake: You need to flip the food or shake the air fryer basket at the halfway mark for even cooking.

13. Grease again: When you are cooking breaded items, spray them with oil one more time during flipping if you notice any dry spots.

14. Stop smoking: You can put a slice of bread under the basket. This will catch any grease that may fall during cooking.

15. Check your food: You need to check your food halfway through the cooking time to make sure your food is cooking nicely.

16. Breading: You need to learn how to bread your food. Air fryer fans blow air at high speed, so you need to

bread your food carefully. If you are not careful, then
armature-style breading will result in uneven cooking.

17. Cool the air fryer basket before cleaning.

An air fryer oven is a little bit different than an air fryer.

Let's discuss the air fryer oven presets. The usual presets are air
fry, toast, pizza, broil, bake, bagel, rotisserie, dehydrate, roast,
reheat, warm, and slow cook. Often air fryer oven heating
elements are located at the top, bottom, and sides. Depending
on the cooking function selected, the unit will use different
heating elements to yield the best result. There are four levels
between the top and bottom heating elements to place your
tray, rack, or pan when cooking.

The first position, near the top heating element, is ideal for
broiling and dehydrating. The second position can be used for
the dehydrate, air fry, broil, bagel, toast, and rotisserie
functions. The third position is best for the dehydrate, pizza,
warm, roast, bake, and reheat functions. Finally, the fourth
position is for the slow cook function.

1. Air fry: The air fry function will use the side heating
   elements with the air fry fans turned on for the entire
   process. You need to place the crisper tray in the
   second position. When cooking foods with a high fat
   content or moisture, it is best to use the pizza rack or
   baking tray below the crisper tray.

2. Toast: The toast function uses the top and bottom heating elements to make the toasted brown color on both sides. You can select how dark your toast should be from levels one to five. You can toast up to six bread slices at a time.

3. Bagel: The bagel function uses the top and bottom heating elements and the air frying fans are turned off during the process. Like the toast function, you can fit up to six slices of bagels and select the desired darkness. The pizza rack is placed in the second position when using this function.

4. Pizza: The pizza function uses the top and bottom heating elements. The bottom heating element makes the dough crispy, while the top cooks the toppings and melts the cheese. The air frying fans may be turned on during the cooking process.

5. Bake: Ideal for baking cakes, pastries, and pies, the bake function uses the top and bottom heating elements and provides the option of turning the air frying fans on or off.

6. Broil: The broil function is ideal for searing and melting cheeses over sandwiches, burgers, or fries. It uses the top heating element while the air frying fan is turned off. The pizza rack must be placed near the top heating element to get the best results.

7. Rotisserie: The rotisserie function uses both the top and bottom heating elements together with the

rotating spit accessory. Food becomes brown and crispy outside while soft and juicy inside.

8. Slow cook: The slow cook function uses the top and bottom heating elements. It is perfect for making tender pulled pork or beef brisket and is best used with a baking dish with a lid or a Dutch oven. Some air fryer ovens are capable of up to 10 hours of slow cooking.

9. Roast: For cooking large cuts of meat, the roast function is the most suitable preset as it evenly cooks the meat on all sides. It also uses the top and bottom heating elements.

10. Dehydrate: The dehydrate function is ideal for drying vegetables, fruits, and meat. It only uses the top heating element with the air fryer fans turned on to evenly dry out the items during the entire process.

11. Reheat: The reheat function uses both the bottom and top heating elements and the air frying fans are turned on. It is ideal for reheating food items without searing them.

12. Warm: The warm function uses the top and bottom heating elements with the air frying fans turned off. It is perfect for keeping food at a safe temperature until you are ready to serve it.

USING YOUR AIR FRYER

Air fryer prep

Before opening an air fryer box:

1. Your air fryer will come with warning cards and warning labels. Read these carefully.
2. Now carefully take your air fryer out of its box and remove all the warning stickers/cards on it.
3. Approach the front of your air fryer and firmly grip the frying basket handle to open the frying basket drawer. Remove the frying basket from your air fryer and palace it on a flat, clean countertop.
4. Ensure that there is no kind of packaging under or around the frying basket drawer.
5. Wash the frying basket and drawer in hot soapy water. Dry all parts well with a kitchen towel.

6. Do not immerse the main air fryer unit in water.

Your first meal

1. Place your air fryer on a kitchen countertop next to a power outlet.
2. Grip the frying basket handle and remove the frying basket. Carefully place it on a flat countertop.
3. Choose your recipe and toss your food into the frying basket. Do not overfill.
4. Put the frying basket back into your air fryer, making sure you hear a nice audible click/lock sound.
5. Plug your air fryer into the nearest power outlet.
6. Follow your recipe instructions and choose an air frying temperature between 175°F and 400°F.
7. Choose a cooking time using the temperature control dial.
8. When cooking is complete, your air fryer may make a beeping noise.
9. Using oven mitts, open the drawer and shake the frying basket vigorously to see if your food is cooked properly.
10. If satisfied, remove the frying basket from your air fryer and place it on a flat countertop.
11. Using kitchen utensils, scoop/take out the food from the frying basket and place it onto a plate.
12. Unplug your air fryer when finished.

Here are things you need to do when you get your first air fryer

Basic steps you need to take

- Plug in the air fryer and preheat it,
- Prepare your food,
- Grease the air fryer basket and place the food in the air fryer basket,
- You can spray a little oil on the food as it will help to make it crispy,
- Close the basket base,
- Set the time and temperature, or you can use any of the presets (such as roast, dehydrate, air fry, etc.),
- Follow the recipe instructions.
- Flip or shake the food at the halfway mark for even cooking.
- If necessary, season the food.
- Press Cancel when you finish cooking.
- Transfer the food from the air fryer basket to a plate.

Additional instructions

- Always use the grate in the basket. This will improve air circulation in the air fryer basket and give you food with very little oil.
- You can check the food during cooking. Pause the machine and remove the basket.

- Then, replace the air fryer basket and turn the appliance back on.

Air frying/Roasting:

- With this setting, you cook your food for a shorter time at a high temperature.
- Roasting foods in the air fryer takes less time than roasting in the oven. The compact size of the air fryer means roasted foods are ready in a shorter time.
- You can roast beef, poultry, and vegetables such as Brussels sprouts, cauliflower florets, broccoli, summer squash, and root vegetables in the air fryer.

Broiling:

- Broiling will help you get a crisp, bubbly top to your dish.
- Ideal for browning a casserole or melting cheese.

Baking:

- You save time when baking in the air fryer. If you are baking a small amount of food or baking during the hot summer days, then an air fryer is ideal.
- A small amount of food cooks better in the air fryer. A

loaf of bread or a full-size cake may not be ideal for the air fryer.

- The air fryer is best for cookies, dinner rolls, and muffins.
- If you are using a traditional air fryer to cook a whole chicken, place the chicken, breast side up, in the air fryer basket. Cook a 3-pound chicken for half an hour. Remove the basket from the air fryer and flip the chicken. Cook for 30 to 40 minutes more until the chicken reaches 165°F.
- For oven-style air fryers: Place the chicken on the roasting rack (breast side up). Place the rack on the lowest level. For a 3-pound chicken, cook for 1 hour. You don't have to flip it. The chicken is done when it reaches 165°F.

Dehydrating:

- If you want to dehydrate foods, then just choose the dehydrating setting. You will get nicely dehydrated food within a short time.
- Ideal for veggie chips, fruit leather, and apple chips.

Reheating:

- Reheating your foods in the air fryer makes them even tastier.

- If the food is frozen, thaw it first.
- Reheat for 3 to 4 minutes at 370°F, then check the food. If necessary, reheat for 2 minutes more.
- Best for fries, chicken tenders/nuggets, smoked or grilled BBQ ribs, tortilla chips, steak, and leftover pizzas.

Dos and Don'ts

1. Don't use too much oil. You don't have to use much oil when cooking in the air fryer.
2. Don't grease the air fryer drawer with cooking spray.
3. Do use vegetable oil. Olive oil has a low smoke point, so avoid using it with air fryer cooking.
4. Don't overfill. Food cooks quickly and comes out crisper if you cook foods in the air fryer in small batches.
5. Do use a spoon or tongs to get cooked food out from the air fryer basket. It will help you to reduce oil on the food.
6. Don't trust the timer 100% because it can be off by a few minutes. Check the food once before the cooking time finishes.
7. Don't put the hot drawer directly on the countertop. Place it on a potholder or a trivet.
8. Do use inserts. You can bake various things when you use inserts.

9. Do bake bread in your air fryer.
10. Don't try to boil water to cook rice or pasta and other grains. You can't cook rice or other grains in an air fryer.

Tips for using the air fryer

1. Choosing a recipe: Choose a recipe that you can cook in your air fryer. Remember that most foods that you can cook in your oven, microwave, or on the stovetop can be cooked in the air fryer, except for those recipes with a lot of fat or liquids.

2. Prepare the air fryer: Read through the recipe to the end to know what accessories you need for cooking. Some recipes call for using the basket, rack, or rotisserie that comes with the air fryer. Other recipes use muffin or cake pans. Just be sure that these pans fit into the fryer and are safe to use.

3. Prepare the ingredients: Gather the ingredients for the recipe and prep them according to the instructions. Once prepped, put the ingredients into the air fryer or in the rack, basket, or pans within the air fryer. Use parchment baking paper or lightly mist with oil spray to prevent food from sticking. Do not overfill or crowd food in the air fryer. Food that is crowded in the air fryer won't cook evenly and can be raw and under-cooked.

4. Setting the temperature and time: Check the recipe and choose the correct temperature and time. You can set it manually, or if you have a digital air fryer, you can press buttons to get your desired temperature and time.

5. Check food during cooking: Checking the food during cooking is a must when using an air fryer. To prevent uneven cooking, you need to shake, flip, or toss the food to distribute it. For some recipes, you will need to turn the food about halfway through when cooking so that it cooks well.

6. Using the basket or rack: Some models of air fryers use layered racks that fit into a square cooking basket. Other models use a round basket for cooking foods.

7. Keep an eye on timing: Air fryers cook at different temperatures depending on what model you have. This is why you need to check the foods during the cooking process to prevent undercooking or overcooking.

8. If you are cooking foods with no fat or lean cuts of meat, then you need to spray oil for a crispy finish and brown coating.

9. Spray pork chops and boneless chicken breasts with oil before seasoning.

10. Freeze foods with wet batter for 10 minutes before placing them in the air fryer.

11. Every machine is a bit different than others. If you can't find your desired control setting, read the manual.

12. Cover the air fryer basket with greased parchment paper for dough and breaded foods.

13. If necessary, use a toothpick to hold food down in the air fryer basket.

14. Use the marinade and juice at the bottom of the drawer as a sauce or baste the food.

Air fryer tricks

1. Preheat your air fryer.

2. Grease your air fryer basket before adding food.

3. Do not use nonstick aerosol cooking sprays.

4. Reheat food in the air fryer to make it crispier and tastier.

5. Use the drippings in the air fryer drawer to make gravies and pan sauces.

6. Shake the air fryer basket a few times for even cooking.

7. Spray the food with oil to achieve the crispiest food.

8. Do not overcrowd your air fryer basket.

9. Do not stack larger items such as pork chops or whole chicken cutlets. Cook them in a single layer.

10. Use parchment paper to make cleanup easier.

11. Coat seasonings with oil before adding them to food items to prevent them from blowing around.

12. After every use, cool the air fryer and clean it.

More air fryer tips

1. Internet recipes are just a guide: Air fryer's operation varies depending on the model. So if you find recipes on the internet, you need to cook them to learn the exact time for your particular model. Check the food a few minutes before the expected cooking time is finished.

2. Reheat foods: Use your air fryer to reheat food. Most foods will take about 5 to 6 minutes to reheat at 400°F.

3. Cooking frozen foods: Yes, you can cook frozen foods in your air fryer.

4. Nonstick surface: You need to protect the nonstick surface of the air fryer. Do not poke or scratch the nonstick surface with sharp objects.

5. Inaccurate preset buttons: Remember that many preset cooking times aren't accurate. Also, these presets do not factor in the weight of the food or how they are sized.

6. Don't overlap meat: When cooking pork chops, steaks, chicken breasts, etc., do not overlap them because stacked food does not cook evenly.

7. Unplug the unit: Do not leave the air fryer plugged in.

8. Toast nuts: The air fryer is an excellent appliance to toast nuts.

9. Have fun and experiment: As you get used to your air fryer, have fun and experiment.

COOKING CHARTS

Internal Temperature Meat Chart:

For maximum food safety, the U.S. Department of Agriculture recommends 160°F for ground lamb, beef, and pork; 165° F for all poultry; and 145° F, with a 3-minute resting period, for all other types of lamb, beef, and pork.

Beef & Veal

- Ground 140°F (70°C)
- Steaks, roasts: medium 145°F (70°C)
- Steaks, roasts: rare 125°F (52°C)

Chicken & Turkey

- Breasts 165°F (75°C)
- Ground, stuffed 165°F (75°C)
- Whole bird, legs, thighs, wings 165°F (75°C)

Fish & Shellfish

- Any type 145°F (63°C)

Lamb

- Ground 160°F (70°C)

- Steaks, roasts: medium 140°F (70°C)
- Steaks, roasts: rare 130°F (55°C)

Pork

- Chops, ground, ribs, roasts 160°F (70°C)
- Fully cooked ham 140°F (60°C)

Air fryer cooking charts

Favorite Frozen foods

Frozen foods	Quantity	Time	Temp	Notes
Breaded shrimp	Up to ½ pound	8 to 10 minutes	400°F	Spray with oil and flip halfway through cooking
Chicken nuggets	6 to 12 pieces	10 to 15 minutes	400°F	Spray with oil and shake halfway through cooking.
Fish fillets	1 to 2 pieces	14 to 15 minutes	400°F	Spray with oil and flip halfway through cooking
Fish sticks	6 to 12 pieces	6 to 10 minutes	400°F	Spray with oil and shake halfway through cooking

Hash browns	1 to 2 pieces	15 to 18 minutes	370°F	Spray with oil and shake halfway through cooking
Onion rings	½ pound	8 to 10 minutes	400°F	Spray with oil and flip halfway through cooking
Tater tots	10 to 20 tots	10 to 12 minutes	400°F	Spray with oil and shake halfway through cooking
Thick fries	10 to 20 fries	18 to 20 minutes	400°F	Spray with oil and shake halfway through cooking
Thin fries	10 to 20 fries	14 minutes	400°F	Spray with oil and shake halfway through cooking
Burgers	1 to 2 patties	14 to 15 minutes	400°F	Do not stack; flip halfway through cooking
Burritos	1 to 2 burritos	8 to 10 minutes	400°F	Spray with oil and flip halfway through cooking
Egg rolls	3 to 4 egg rolls	3 to 6 minutes	390°F	Brush or spray with oil before cooking
Meatballs	5 to 10 meatballs	8 to 10 minutes	380°F	Flip halfway through cooking

Mozzarella sticks	4 to 8 sticks	8 to 10 minutes	360°F	Spray with olive oil and flip halfway through cooking
Pizza	½ pizza	5 to 10 minutes	390°F	Place pizza on parchment paper; make sure it fits in the basket
Pizza bagels	2 to 3 pizza bagels	8 to 10 minutes	375°F	Spray with oil; do not stack
Pizza rolls (bites)	5 to 10 pizza rolls	5 to 7 minutes	375°F	Spray with oil and shake halfway through cooking
Potstickers	5 to 10 pot stickers	8 to 10 minutes	400°F	Spray with oil and flip halfway through cooking
Samosas	3 to 4 samosas	5 to 10 minutes	400°F	Spray with oil and shake halfway through cooking

Fresh foods

Fresh vegetables	Quantity	Time	Temp	Notes
Asparagus	½ pound	5 to 8 minutes	400°F	Trim ends before cooking; spray with oil and sprinkle with seasonings
Broccoli	1 to 2 cups	5 to 8 minutes	400°F	Spray with oil and sprinkle with seasonings
Brussels sprouts	1 cup	13 to 15 minutes	380°F	Trim bottoms and cut in half before cooking; spray with oil and sprinkle with seasonings
Carrots	½ to 1 cup	7 to 10 minutes	380°F	Cut first; spray with oil and sprinkle with seasonings

Cauliflower florets	1 to 2 cups	9 to 10 minutes	360°F	Spray with oil and sprinkle with seasonings
Corn on the cob	2 ears	6 minutes	390°F	Spray with oil and sprinkle with seasonings
Eggplant	½ to 2 pounds	13 to 15 minutes	400°F	Cut into slices; spray with oil and flip halfway through cooking
Green beans	½ to 1 pound	5 minutes	400°F	Trim ends; spray with oil and shake halfway through cooking
Kale	½ bunch	10 to 12 minutes	275°F	Trim leaves from the ribs; spray with oil and sprinkle with seasonings

Mushrooms	½ to 1 cup	5 to 8 minutes	400°F	Trim stems first; sprinkle with seasonings
Onions	½ to 1 pound	5 to 8 minutes	370°F	Cut first
Peppers (bell)	½ to 1 cup	6 to 8 minutes	370°F	Cut first
Potatoes (baked)	1 to 2 pounds	40 minutes	400°F	Poke holes first; spray with oil and sprinkle with seasonings
Potatoes (cubed)	1 to 2 cups	15 minutes	400°F	Spray with oil and shake halfway through cooking
Potatoes (fries)	1 to 2 cups	15 minutes	380°F	Spray with oil and shake halfway through cooking

Potatoes (wedges)	1 to 3 cups	18 to 20 minutes	380°F	Spray with oil and shake halfway through cooking
Squash	½ pound	12 to 13 minutes	400°F	Spray with oil and sprinkle with seasonings
Sweet potatoes (baked)	1 large or 2 small sweet potatoes	35 to 40 minutes	390°F	Poke holes first; spray with oil and sprinkle with seasonings
Sweet potatoes (cubed)	1 to 3 cups	14 to 20 minutes	380°F	Spray with oil and shake halfway through cooking
Sweet (fries) potatoes	1 to 2 cups	25 minutes	380°F	Spray with oil and shake halfway through
Tomatoes (breaded)	1 to 2 tomatoes	10 minutes	350°F	Cut first; season or bread, and spray with oil

Zucchini	½ to 1 pound	10 to 12 minutes	370°F	Cut first; spray with oil and sprinkle with seasonings

Chicken	Quantity	Time	Temp	Notes
Chicken breasts (boneless, skinless)	1 to 2 (6-ounce) breasts	12 to 15 minutes	380°F	Spray with oil, sprinkle with seasonings and flip halfway through cooking
Chicken drumettes	Up to 4 drumettes	20 minutes	400°F	Spray with oil, sprinkle with seasonings and shake halfway through cooking
Chicken drumsticks	1 to 4 drumsticks	16 to 20 minutes	390°F	Spray with oil, sprinkle with seasonings and shake halfway through cooking
Chicken thighs	1 to 2 (6-ounce) thighs	22 minutes	380°F	Spray with oil, sprinkle with seasonings and flip

(bone-in)				halfway through cooking
Chicken thighs (boneless)	1 to 2 (6-ounce) thighs	18 to 20 minutes	380°F	Spray with oil, sprinkle with seasonings and flip halfway through cooking
Chicken tenders	Up to 4 tenders	8 to 10 minutes	375°F	Spray with oil, sprinkle with seasonings and shake halfway through cooking
Chicken wings	Up to 4 wings	15 to 20 minutes	400°F	Spray with oil, sprinkle with seasonings and shake halfway through cooking
Whole chicken	1 pound	75 minutes	360°F	Spray with oil, sprinkle with seasonings

Beef	Quantity	Time	Temp	Notes
Burgers	1 to 2 patties	8 to 10 minutes	400°F	Do not stack; flip halfway through cooking
Filet mignon	1 to 2 (6 ounce) steaks	8 to 10 minutes	360°F	Time varies depending on the desired doneness; 125°F for rare, 135°F for medium-rare, 160°F for well-done
Flank steak	¼ to ½ pound	8 to 10 minutes	360°F	Time will vary depending on the desired doneness; 125°F for rare, 135°F for medium-rare, 160°F for well-done
Meatballs	5 to 10 meatballs	7 to 10 minutes	380°F	Sprinkle with seasoning and flip

				halfway through cooking
Ribeye	1 to 2 (6-ounce) steaks	10 to 15 minutes	380°F	Time will vary depending on the desired doneness; 125°F for rare, 135°F for medium-rare, 160°F for well done
Sirloin steak	1 to 2 (6-ounce) steaks	12 to 14 minutes	400°F	Time will vary depending on the desired doneness; 125°F for rare, 135°F for medium-rare, 160°F for well-done

Pork and Lamb	Quantity	Time	Temp	Notes
Bacon	2 to 4 slices	7 to 10 minutes	400°F	Flip halfway through cooking
Lamb chops	1 to 2 (3-ounce) chops	10 to 12 minutes	400°F	Do not stack; sprinkle with seasonings and flip halfway through cooking
Pork chops (bone-in or boneless)	1 to 2 (3-ounce) chops	12 to 15 minutes	380°F	Spray with oil, sprinkle with seasonings and flip halfway through cooking
Pork loin	¼ to ½ pound	50 to 60 minutes	360°F	Spray with oil, sprinkle with seasonings and flip halfway through cooking
Pork tenderloin	¼ to ½ pound	12 to 15 minutes	390°F	Spray with oil, sprinkle with seasonings and cook whole

Rack of lamb	¼ to ½ pound	22 to 25 minutes	380°F	Do not stack; flip halfway through cooking
Sausage (links)	5 to 10 links	13 to 15 minutes	380°F	Pierce holes in the sausage first
Sausage (patties)	1 to 4 patties	13 to 15 minutes	380°F	Flip halfway through cooking

Fish and Seafood	Quantity	Time	Temp	Notes
Crab cakes	1 to 2 cakes	8 to 10 minutes	375°F	Toss with cornstarch; spray with oil and sprinkle with seasonings
Fish fillets	¼ to ½ pound	10 to 12 minutes	320°F	Spray with oil; sprinkle with seasonings
Scallops	¼ to ½ pound	5 to 7 minutes	320°F	Spray with oil; sprinkle with seasonings

Shrimp	¼ to ½ pound	7 to 8 minutes	400°F	Peel and devein; spray with oil and sprinkle with seasonings

Fresh fruit	Quantity	Time	Temp	Notes
Apples	1 to 3 cups	4 to 7 minutes	350°F	Cut first; peel if desired
Bananas	1 to 3 cups	4 to 7 minutes	350°F	Peel and cut first
Peaches	1 to 3 cups	5 to 6 minutes	350°F	Cut first

Measurement conversions

US Standard	US Standard (Ounces)	Metric (Approximate)
2 tablespoons	1 fl. oz.	30 mL
¼ cup	2 fl. oz.	60 mL
½ cup	4 fl. oz.	120 mL
1 cup	8 fl. oz.	240 mL
1 ½ cups	12 fl. oz.	355 mL
2 cups or 1 pint	16 fl. oz.	475 mL
4 cups or 1 quart	32 fl. oz.	1 L
1 gallon	128 fl. oz.	4 L

Oven Temperatures

Fahrenheit	Celsius
250°F	120°C
300°F	150°C
325°F	165°C
350°F	180°C
375°F	190°C
400°F	200°C
425°F	220°C
450°F	230°C

5

CARING FOR AND MAINTAINING YOUR AIR FRYER

Control dials

1. The temperature control dial allows you to select the frying temperature. Temperatures can be adjusted at any time before or during the cooking period.

2. The control panel shows the Heat On light when the cooking temperature is reached. It also shows the red Power light, which will turn on when you use your fryer. The shortcut functions are specifically designed for certain kinds of food, like poultry and fish.

3. The automatic timer button allows you to select how long your food will cook for and will automatically count down during the cooking period. Most air fryers turn off automatically, but you should always check and turn both the

temperature control dial and the timer dial to O (off).

Clean up

- Air fryer parts are usually dishwasher-safe, but ideally, you should hand wash theparts to prevent wear and tear on the dishwasher.
- You need to clean your air fryer after every use.
- Before cleaning, first unplug the air fryer and wait 30 minutes for the parts to cool down.
- If you used a marinade or sticky sauce, then clean the parts while they are still warm.
- Once cool, wipe out oil from the drawer.
- Wash the drawer, basket, and tray with hot soapy water and a regular kitchen sponge.
- Soak the parts in soapy water to remove stuck-on food.
- You can use a vinegar and water solution or a baking soda and water paste to get rid of grease build-up.
- Rinse the basket and drawer with clean water to remove soap.
- Clean out grease from any grooves or nooks with a wooden skewer.
- Use a damp cloth to wipe down the insides and heating element.
- Use a damp cloth or sponge to wipe down the outside of the air fryer after each use. This will remove any

food particles or grease that may have latched on during cooking
- Once you finish cleaning the air fryer, run it for a few minutes to dry out the inside.
- Ensure that the drawer and basket are dry before assembling them.

Cleaning tips

- Abrasive materials or cleaners can damage the nonstick coating of your basket and drawer. So avoid using them.
- Do not use utensils to remove stuck-on food from your air fryer parts. It can damage the nonstick coating.
- If you are cooking foods in batches, wait until you finish cooking to clean your air fryer.

Deep cleaning

- Soak the pan and the basket in hot soapy water for 10 to 15 minutes.
- Flip the air fryer and clean the bottom part with a damp microfiber cloth.
- Create a paste with 1 part blue Dawn dishwashing soap, 1 part baking soda, 1 part vinegar or hydrogen

peroxide. Use this paste to scrub the insides of the air fryer with a toothbrush.

- Use a microfiber cloth to wipe off the solution from the air fryer. Then continue to scrub with the toothbrush until you remove all the stuck-on food.
- Allow to sit for a few minutes, then rinse the parts with clean water to remove any soap. Clean between every grate in the basket with cotton swabs.
- Wipe each grate with a microfiber cloth.
- Using a scrubbing pad is another good idea.
- Clean the fan vents with a cotton swab.
- Allow the air fryer and its parts to dry overnight before using it again.

Effective tips to maintain an air fryer

- Check the cords before you plug it in. If the cords are even slightly damaged, it will result in serious problems.
- Your kitchen counter should be cleaned before you use it. There shouldn't be any water or food crumbs on it.
- Check the inside basket of the air fryer. If it has been a long since you used your air fryer, make sure there is no dust, debris, or leftover food residue. Clean the pan before you use it.
- Always place the air fryer on a level surface.

- Your air fryer gets hot. Do not touch any of its surfaces when it's cooking. When cooking is complete, use oven mitts or potholders to touch it and wait for it to cool down.

- Avoid immersing the cord, plug, or the air fryer unit in water or other liquid due to possibility of electric shock.

- Persons with reduced sensory, physical, or mental abilities, or lack of experience and knowledge, should not use air fryer without supervision.

- Avoid using your air fryer outdoors due to adverse weather conditions.

- Avoid letting the cord hang over the edge of the table or countertop, especially if you have pets in the house.

- Avoid placing your air fryer near a hot gas or electric burner.

- Ensure that both the timer dial and temperature dial are off before disconnecting your air fryer from the power outlet.

- Ensure that the frying basket is locked into position when turning on your air fryer.

- Ensure that the frying basket drawer is fully closed and the handle locked securely in the drawer when using your air fryer.

- Handle your air fryer carefully after frying because the basket and the food inside of it are extremely hot.

Storing your air fryer

- If you use your air fryer regularly, keep it on the countertop for easy access.
- Do not place your air fryer near the stovetop or oven.
- Do not store air fryer tools inside the appliance. It may cause accidents if you start the air fryer while the tools are inside.
- Clean the air fryer thoroughly before storing it. Wait 30 minutes after use before cleaning.
- When storing your air fryer, make sure the appliance is in an upright position. Make sure the power cable is not plugged into a wall outlet.

Maintenance

- Check the air fryer cord regularly. If the cord is damaged, then take the appliance to a mechanic. Never plug a damaged cord into an outlet.
- Before using your air fryer, make sure the unit is clean and free of any debris. Check inside before starting the appliance.
- If the inside is not clean, clean the air fryer before using it.
- Place the air fryer on a level surface before starting.
- Regularly check each component of the air fryer. If you notice any part is damaged, contact the manufacturer.

- Follow the user manual's instructions when cooking food in the air fryer.

Safety tips

1. Do not buy a cheap, low-quality air fryer
2. Do not place it on an uneven surface
3. Do not overcrowd the basket
4. Do not leave the appliance unattended
5. Read the manual before using the air fryer
6. Clean the appliance after every use
7. Do not wash the electrical components
8. Use the right amount of oil — your air fryer needs only a little oil, so do not use too much
9. Grease the air fryer basket to prevent food from getting stuck and prevent potential burning and smoking
10. Dry your hands before touching the air fryer
11. Make sure accessories are safe for use with an air fryer
12. Shake the basket or flip the food during the middle of the cooking process to ensure even cooking

If your air fryer needs repairing, seek professional support.

6

FREQUENTLY ASKED QUESTIONS

TROUBLESHOOTING

The air fryer is not switching on.

You should see a green light or similar indicator when the air fryer is on. A red light indicates that the fryer is heating up. If your air fryer is not starting, then you should:

- Turn the timer knob and set it to preheat for 3 minutes.
- Check if you inserted the plug correctly. Also, notice if the air fryer is getting power from the cord.

During use, the outside of the air fryer is hot.

- It is normal for the outside of the unit to get hot during operation. While the air fryer is in use, only touch the buttons and handles.
- Place the air fryer on a spot where children can't reach it.

White smoke is coming from the air fryer.

Cooking materials can cause white smoke to rise from the air fryer. If you notice this happening, then:

- Turn off the air fryer and remove the pan.
- Remove the basket from the pan and use a cloth or paper towel to soak up the oil from the pan.
- Once you have finished cleaning, reassemble the fryer and start again.
- Put some water in the drawer underneath the food if cooking fatty foods like bacon or meatballs to reduce smoking.

Blue or black smoke is coming out of the air fryer.

- Black smoke is usually due to burned food. You need to clean the air fryer after every use. If you do not, the remaining food particles will burn when you use the appliance again. Turn the machine off and cool it completely. Then check it for burned food.

- If no food is burning, but you notice black smoke, it is an electrical issue.
- Disconnect the air fryer and take it to an electrician.

The air fryer smells funny or smell smoke while air frying.

- Often a dirty air fryer causes smoke during cooking.
- If you notice burning small but your food is not burning, clean the air fryer properly to remove built-up residue.

There is an odor after cleaning the air fryer.

- Soak the air fryer basket in soapy water for an hour.
- Another option is to slice a lemon in half, then rub the air fryer drawer and basket with one half and let them sit for 30 minutes. Then rewash.

The air fryer doesn't turn on.

- If the timer is running, air fryers don't turn on. So check out the timer.
- Check that the drawer is inserted properly.

The air fryer keeps turning off.

- Check the power cord. Make sure your air fryer is getting power.
- Check if the power cord is damaged. Make sure the power cord is inserted correctly in the outlet.
- If the power cord is okay, check the circuit breaker.
- Check all the air fryer parts to make sure there are no faulty components and that nothing is damaged.
- If you can't fix it, then contact customer service.

There are bubbles or peeling on the inside of the appliance.

- If you accidentally scratched the inside of the air fryer and damaged the nonstick coating, you might notice bubbling during cooking.
- If you notice bubbling of the lining, contact customer service and see if you can get a warranty replacement.

Food is not cooking properly.

- Follow the recipe exactly. Check if you have overcrowded the ingredients. This is the main reason that food does not cook evenly in an air fryer.

The appliance won't stop.

- The air fryer fan operates at high speed and needs some time to stop. Do not worry, it will stop soon.

The reasons why your air fryer isn't heating up

Here are the steps you need to take to fix this problem.

1. Check the outlet of the air fryer: Often, the reason is a silly one. If it doesn't start, check to see if you plugged in your air fryer! Sometimes the plug gets knocked out of the socket and your air fryer doesn't start. If the air fryer is plugged in, check if the fuse is blown. This often happens if you have too many devices plugged into one outlet. Breakers often flip when you plug in several appliances like waffle makers, toaster ovens, and others into a single outlet. This overloads the socket and turns it off. To know if the fuse has blown, plug in an appliance that works; if it doesn't turn on, then the fuse is blown. Unplug the devices from the outlet and switch the breaker back on.

2. Power cord: If you didn't find any issues with the outlet itself, check the power cord to see if it is damaged. You may face this problem, especially if you brought a cheap air fryer. Look for any signs of fraying or breakage. If it is a low-quality power cord, there is a chance that it's been damaged because of excess

movement or overuse. Make sure you are handling power cords carefully because they can break when they are not handled properly. Mice or other pests can also cause damage to the power cord. If you store your air fryer in a dark place without a box, there is a chance that rats may have chewed the cord and damaged it. Lastly, if the cord isn't damaged, then it might have detached from the air fryer itself. If this happens, you have to take the air fryer to an electrician.

3. The temperature setting: If you couldn't find any issues with the power outlet or the power cord, then see if the problem is caused by one of the external settings. First, take a look at the temperature setting. Different brands of air fryers have slightly different temperature settings. Some air fryers have buttons. Some have a dial. If the air fryer is set on a low setting (104°F/40°C), you need to turn the temperature up so that the air fryer works properly. If your air fryer has a digital temperature setting, make sure you are pressing the right settings. Selecting a lower temperature won't heat up the air fryer enough.

4. Air fryer timer: Some air fryers won't start up if you didn't set a time with the timer setting. Depending on the model, the timer setting is also different. For example, if you have a digital model, you can just punch the time into it. If you have an analog machine, you have to turn the dial to set the correct time.

5. The air fryer door: Once you know that that timer and temperature settings are okay, it is time to look at the door or lid of your air fryer. Similar to an oven, an air fryer will leak heat if it isn't sealed correctly. Old-style air fryers will heat slightly if the door is open or not sealed tightly. The newer model air fryers won't even start if the door is not locked. Make sure the lid or door is perfectly sealed if the air fryer won't start.

6. The amount of food you put in the basket: If you overfill the air fryer basket, you run the risk of overloading the air fryer. This also means that the heat won't distribute evenly. So check to make sure that you haven't overfilled your air fryer basket. There is a "Max" marker in the air fryer basket. Never cross that mark. For example, if you fill up your air fryer with a big bag of frozen French fries, you will notice that your air fryer isn't heating up as expected. The basket needs to have enough empty room so the hot air can circulate. This will prevent the air fryer from heating up.

7. The heating element: If you can't find the fault after checking all the above, you need to check the heating element. The heating element creates the heat that cooks your food. This is an important part of your air fryer, and you need to be careful when taking a peek at it. If you are a novice, it is wise to call customer care instead of you poking and prodding around.

COOKING

Do you need to use oil with the air fryer?

- You just have to spray a bit of oil so the food doesn't get stuck in the air fryer basket, and food gets that golden brown color you want.

What should I avoid cooking in the air fryer?

- Do not cook foods that require water, such as grains and rice. If you are using batter, freeze the battered food first to make it hard. Then bake in the air fryer.

Why do I have to shake the air fryer basket?

- You need to shake the air fryer basket or flip the food for even cooking.

Why don't some types of foods turn out crispy?

- Usually, vegetables will not get a crunchy outer layer.
- Coating food items with bread crumbs will give them an extra crunch.
- Do not overcrowd the cooking basket. It will prevent crunchiness.

Can I steam in the air fryer?

- No, you can't steam foods in the air fryer. You need to heat the water from below to steam, but the air fryer heats the food from the above.

Why do I have overcooked or burned food?

- Check your food several times during the cooking process to prevent this from happening.
- If you cook food in batches, you need to check the second batch of foods earlier because the air fryer will already be hot and will cook the second and third batches of food faster.

Do I need to preheat the air fryer?

- Preheating can help you cut down on cooking time.

How much can an air fryer hold?

- We discussed a variety of air fryers in the second chapter. Choose one that suits your needs.

How do I prevent foods from getting stuck to the air fryer basket?

- You need to spray a bit of oil on your food to prevent sticking. Using parchment paper also helps.

How do I safely remove foods from the air fryer?

- Finish cooking, then remove the air fryer basket from the air fryer.
- Use a pair of tongs to remove food safely from the basket.

Can I cook different foods in the air fryer?

- Yes, you can cook different foods in your air fryer. You can use it for cooking different types of foods like casseroles and even desserts.

How much food can I put inside?

- Different air fryers have different capacities. To know how much food you can put in, look for the "Max" mark and use it as a guide to filling the basket.

Can I add extra ingredients during the cooking process?

- Yes, you can. Just open the air fryer and add ingredients. There is no need to change the internal temperature to stabilize once you close the air fryer chamber.

Can I put aluminum or baking paper at the bottom of the air fryer?

- Yes, you can use either to line the base of the air fryer. However, make sure that you poke holes so that the hot air can pass through the material and cook food properly.

Why does it take the food more time to cook?

- Your pieces of meat or vegetables are larger than the recipe calls for.
- You are using a deeper cake pan than specified.
- You are doubling the recipe.

Why is the food only partly cooked?

- You need to cook food in one layer in batches.

SAFEGUARDS

1. Keep your hands away from the steam outlets of the air fryer.

2. Immediately disconnect the appliance if you notice dark smoke initiating from the air fryer.

3. Do not submerge the air fryer in water.

4. Never overcrowd or overfill your air fryer because it can cause damage.

5. Don't touch the inside of your air fryer while it is in use.

6. Read the manual. You must read the manual.

7. Check that you are using the right power source and outlet. Otherwise, problems can happen.

8. Check the assembly of the appliance.

9. Follow the right procedures. Read the cooking instructions carefully and follow them.

10. Do not use harsh chemicals and cleaners on the air fryer.

11. Do not wash the air fryer immediately after use. Wait 30 minutes.

AIR FRYERS AND DIETS

Air Fryers and Diets

Whether you follow the Ketogenic diet, the Mediterranean diet, or the Vegan diet, using an air fryer is the best way to cook your food.

Let's discuss the diets.

The Mediterranean Lifestyle

The Mediterranean diet is not just a diet, it is a lifestyle — a healthy, active, and emotionally rich lifestyle. Diet is certainly a big part of what makes the Mediterranean region healthy. However, the overall lifestyle of the Mediterranean people is also important to the success of this eating plan. The people who live in the Mediterranean basin have a very different approach to life. Many often walk or cycle to work, making their days more active and increasing their physical wellbeing.

People typically enjoy relaxed meals with their families, often accompanied by red wine. Each meal is seen as a feast, and food is made and enjoyed together. Families and friends sit down to enjoy and celebrate meals such as breakfast, lunch, and dinner, and the food is never rushed. This time spent eating with family and friends gives you daily doses of healthy social interaction and contributes to feeling emotionally satiated. Mediterranean buy fresh, locally grown produce from neighborhood shops and markets, and stop to chat with neighbors and friends while doing their errands.

Instead of spending hours commuting in traffic, they spend their time out and about in town. Instead of eating lunch hunched over their office computer, most people walk home to enjoy a meal with their families. The Mediterranean diet is a wholesome diet that is full of flavors and colors. It will not only leave you satiated but also leave you feeling healthy and more physically wealthy when followed correctly.

The ten directives of the Mediterranean Diet

1. Eat a wide variety of fresh, non-processed food
2. Avoid refined sugar, saturated fat, trans fat, and excess sodium
3. Avoid butter and margarine and consume olive oil
4. Limit portion size

5. Drink an adequate amount of water

6. Consume alcohol in moderation

7. Exercise daily, a minimum of 30 minutes per day

8. Abstain from smoking

9. Relax, especially after meals

10. Laugh, smile, and enjoy life

The top ten tips for your success:

1. Active lifestyle: The Mediterranean lifestyle encourages eating healthy foods, but exercise and an active lifestyle are also a big part of their way of life. At home, you can play with your kids, clean the house or yard, walk with your dog in the park, skate, or ride a bike more and drive less, and take the stairs instead of using the elevator. Park your car farther from the shopping mall when you go shopping. If possible, walk, and take the longer route.

2. Enjoy your meals with family: Start planning family dinners more often, at least twice a week. Besides having fun moments, you will also bring some benefits to your health. Don't just pick up some fast food to bring home; get your children involved and spend a great time together cooking a healthy, homemade meal. This will give you a chance to become more creative.

3. Substitute butter with healthy oils: Always use extra

virgin olive oil instead of butter or margarine. If your recipe includes an unhealthy fat, replace it with the same quantity of olive oil. This will be beneficial for your heart, and at the same time, the dish will become even more delicious.

4. Use more spices and herbs; use less salt: Herbs and spices are rich in antioxidants. They raise the nutrition value of meals and reduce sodium levels. Additionally, researchers have revealed that salt increases blood pressure. You can use a limited amount of sea salt.

5. Use plant-focused recipes: Meat is the main focus in dishes in the U.S., but the Mediterranean diet encourages using more vegetables. Fruits and vegetables are the core components of this eating pattern, so it is better to put them in the middle of your plate rather than on the side. Choose fruit as dessert. Use brown sugar or honey to add some flavors. Instead of crackers or chips, eat fresh fruit as a snack.

6. Consume more fish instead of red meat: The Mediterranean diet recommends eating more fish instead of red meat. Fatty fish like salmon, herring, sardines, and tuna are rich in omega-3 fatty acids and have anti-inflammatory properties.

7. Eat more legumes: Legumes are a crucial part of the Mediterranean diet. They are a great substitute for meat. Beans are high in minerals and antioxidants and are a huge source of protein and fiber.

8. Avoid refined flour and use whole grains: Avoid white bread and white rice. Try barley, quinoa, or millet.

9. Eat seasonal foods: Shop at the local farmers market for fresh seasonal products. Make eating a special ritual, and don't let yourself eating in front of the TV or while surfing the web.

10. Drink alcohol in moderation: Drink moderately and only focus on drinking red wine. Try not to drink outside of mealtime.

THE MEDITERRANEAN DIET PYRAMID

Mediterranean Diet Pyramid

1. Whole grains, vegetables, and fruits: They are an integral part of the Mediterranean diet plan. The grains you should add to your diet should be non-refined whole grains such as quinoa and brown rice. Vegetables can include green leafy vegetables such as kale, spinach, broccoli, Brussels sprouts, cauliflower, and carrots.

2. Olive oil: Olive oil is a very important part of the Mediterranean diet and much healthier than other vegetable oils such as canola or sunflower oil. Use olive oil with every dish and replace butter and margarine with olive oil. Consume an average of ½ cup per week.

3. Legumes, nuts, and seeds: Beans, lentils, nuts, and

seeds are a great source of protein. Use these ingredients and substitute them for red meat where possible. They are a more filling, more affordable, and healthier protein source than red meats.

4. Spices: Use herbs and spices to flavor food instead of sodium-rich table salt. Get creative when flavoring food by combining fresh herbs with olive oil to marinate your food. Make seasonal dishes with fresh-cracked black pepper for extra spiciness.

5. Fish and seafood: The omega-3 oils found in fish is required for healthy brain development, and regular consumption helps reduce the risk of cardiovascular disease.

6. Poultry, eggs, cheese, and yogurt: Include poultry, eggs, cheese, and yogurt in your daily diet. Always focus on moderate consumption of any dairy products and monitor their effects on you.

7. Meats: Red meat should be kept to a minimum as it is not the healthiest diet option and can be replaced by legumes, nuts, and seeds. When you eat red meat, try to eat grass-fed, organic meat and keep it to a minimum number of servings per week.

8. Red wine: Many studies have shown that one glass of red wine per day can have multiple beneficial aspects for your health. It is recommended on the Mediterranean diet to enjoy one glass of red wine.

Remember, more than two glasses can be detrimental to your health.

9. Physical activity and social interaction: The Mediterranean lifestyle includes moderate amounts of daily physical activity and social interaction. Mediterranean people walk or cycle to work and lead very active lifestyles. Meals are also enjoyed as a family and are eaten over a longer period of time, with plenty of conversation and laughs in between. If you cannot walk or cycle to work, try to take short walks when home and incorporate physical activity into your normal day, such as taking the stairs instead of the elevator. Sit down at breakfast, lunch, and dinner and take time to savor your food. Try to taste every bite and identify the ingredients. Use dinnertime to talk to your family and discuss everyone's day, goals for the week, your hobbies, and anything interesting you may have seen or heard that day.

On the Mediterranean diet, you need to consume:

1. At least 4 servings of fresh fruits and vegetables per day
2. 3 to 5 servings of whole grains per day
3. 4 to 6 servings of healthful fats per day
4. At least 3 servings of fish and seafood per week
5. Up to 7 servings of dairy products per week

6. Up to 1 five-ounce glass of red wine daily for women,
   2 glasses daily for men
7. 3 to 5 servings of eggs per week (6 to 10 eggs)
8. 2 to 5 servings of poultry per week
9. Up to 4 servings of sweets per week
10. 3 to 5 servings of red meat per month

The Mediterranean diet offers many health benefits:

1. Weight loss: For many people who follow it, the Mediterranean diet results in weight loss naturally and effortlessly. While most popular weight-loss diets emphasize counting calories, following a strict menu, weighing and measuring foods, or starting a demanding exercise program, this diet focuses on consuming a wide variety of healthful foods. By removing processed foods and fast foods from your diet (they are loaded with unhealthy fats, sugar, and chemicals), you significantly lower your calorie intake while eating more foods. Without counting fat grams or calories, you trade unhealthful, "empty" foods for those that promote good health and support the loss of stored fat. The Mediterranean diet includes a wide variety of healthful, fresh foods that supply fiber and good fats which supports weight loss by helping you to feel full. A high-fiber diet also slows the rate at which sugar is absorbed into your bloodstream, which helps control both blood sugar and insulin levels. As insulin triggers fat storage, too much insulin in the bloodstream stops fat loss. Fiber from fruits, whole grains, and vegetables also helps to improve digestion, which can be an important factor in weight loss. Many antioxidants found in fresh fruits and vegetables (such as lutein in apples) can encourage weight loss. Overall, the Mediterranean diet allows people to lose weight naturally and healthily, without going hungry or eliminating food groups.

https://www.nejm.org/doi/full/10.1056/NEJMoa0708681

2. Improves heart health: Studies show that the healthy monounsaturated fat and omega-3 fat-rich Mediterranean diet lowers the risk of heart disease. The following studies show that consuming olive oil can lower the risk of sudden cardiac death by 45% and the risk of cardiac death by 30%.

https://www.ncbi.nlm.nih.gov/pubmed/17058434

https://www.ncbi.nlm.nih.gov/pubmed/23939686

3. Helps fight cancer: A diet that includes lots of fresh vegetables and fruits can prevent cell mutation, lowers inflammation, protects DNA from damage, fights cancer, and delays tumor growth.

https://www.ncbi.nlm.nih.gov/pubmed/22644232

4. Prevents and treats diabetes: In addition to other benefits, the Mediterranean diet is also an anti-inflammatory diet. This means that the diet can reduce the risk of diseases that are caused by inflammation, such as metabolic syndrome and type 2 diabetes.

https://www.ncbi.nlm.nih.gov/pubmed/19689829

5. Improves cognitive health and can improve mood:
The Mediterranean diet acts as a natural Alzheimer's and Parkinson's disease treatment because the healthy fats included are good for your brain. Anti-inflammatory fruits, vegetables, and healthy fats like olive oil and nuts are known to fight age-related cognitive decline. They also prevent the harmful effects of free radical damage and toxicity. Both of these reduce brain function.

https://www.ncbi.nlm.nih.gov/pmc/articles/PMC5538737/

https://www.ncbi.nlm.nih.gov/pubmed/16622828

https://www.ncbi.nlm.nih.gov/pubmed/19262590

6. Strengthens bones: Olive oil can help your bones stay strong. A study shows that following the Mediterranean diet can help prevent osteoporosis.

https://www.ncbi.nlm.nih.gov/pubmed/24975408

https://www.ncbi.nlm.nih.gov/pubmed/22946650

7. Good for your gut: Research shows that dieters who follow the Mediterranean diet have a higher percentage of good bacteria in their gut. Research also shows that eating more plant-based foods such as vegetables, fruits, and legumes boosts good bacteria production.

https://www.frontiersin.org/articles/10.3389/fnut.2018.00028/ful

8. Lowers anxiety and fights depression: Doctors suggest the Mediterranean diet as a treatment for patients with depression, anxiety, and other mental health issues. Food items such as kale, spinach, and eggs contain carotenoids. This substance boosts the good bacteria in your gut and improves mood.

https://www.practiceupdate.com/content/healthy-dietary-choices-may-reduce-the-risk-of-depression/74278

https://www.ncbi.nlm.nih.gov/pubmed/29775747

9. Helps you to live longer: Eating the Mediterranean diet can help you live longer. Studies show that monounsaturated fat is linked with lower levels of inflammatory disease such as depression, cancer, heart disease, cognitive deterioration, and Alzheimer's disease.

https://www.ahajournals.org/doi/pdf/10.1161/01.cir.99.6.779

10. Good for post-menopausal women: Menopause can trigger bone and muscle loss. The Mediterranean diet can have a positive impact.

https://www.sciencedaily.com/releases/2018/03/180318144826.htm

Key benefits of using an air fryer for cooking while on the Mediterranean diet

1. The Mediterranean diet calls for food with less oil, and you can achieve that with the air fryer.
2. Fruit is one of the main ingredients of the Mediterranean diet. You can use the air fryer for cooking a variety of fruit dessert recipes.
3. The Mediterranean diet asks you to avoid refined sugar, saturated fat, trans fat, and excess sodium. You can achieve all these by using an air fryer.
4. The Mediterranean diet requires you to eat less meat and more vegetables. You can use your air fryer to cook more tasty vegetable dishes and reduce your need to eat more red meat.

THE KETOGENIC DIET

The Ketogenic diet is a low-carb, moderate protein, and high-fat diet. The diet is a proven weight loss tool and offers other health benefits. The diet was introduced in the 1920s to treat epilepsy in children. In the early 1990s, this diet became popular as a weight loss diet. It reduces or eliminates all the food that converts into sugar/blood glucose in the body. With a standard diet, all carbohydrate and sugar-rich foods we consume convert to blood glucose/sugar.

How the Ketogenic diet works

The human body can use several food sources for fuel. Carbohydrates are your body's first choice because they are easily accessible. Once you eat a carb/sugar-rich food, it quickly gets converted to blood glucose in the body. Additional blood glucose signals your pancreas to produce insulin. Insulin's job is to carry the blood glucose into cells in the body to be used as energy. Some blood glucose is used, and the additional amounts get stored as body fat. Usually, we overeat when eating a carb and sugar-rich meal because they make us feel good, and are not filling/satisfying like fat. Eating a small amount of carb and sugar-rich food doesn't satisfy us. This is the reason we often overeat. Eating carb-rich food triggers insulin production. Insulin transports blood glucose to the cells. Also, insulin prevents any fat cell breakdown. So with carb-rich diets, we never lose weight.

On the other hand, a low carb, high-fat Keto diet takes advantage of our body's natural system that uses fat for fuel. Unlike carbs and sugar, fat has a very filling presence, so your hunger is easily quashed. You eat high fat, low carb meals with keto, so your body can't use blood glucose as fuel. It is forced to use both fat that you eat and any existing body fat as fuel. Eating fat-rich foods does not trigger insulin production, so your body can start to break down body fat for energy. This state is called ketosis. When you restrict carbs, your liver starts to produce ketones (also known as ketone bodies). They are transported from the liver to the whole body to use as energy. With the Keto diet, your aim is to reach the state of ketosis.

The standard Ketogenic diet macronutrient requirements are as follows:

- 60 to 75% calories from fat
- 20 to 30% calories from protein
- 5 to 10% calories from carbohydrates

What You Can and Can't Eat on a Keto Diet

You can eat from the following food groups:

- Fats and oils: Get your fats from meat and nuts. Supplement with monounsaturated and saturated fats like olive oil, butter, and coconut oil.
- Protein: Whenever possible, eat grass-fed, pasture-raised, organic meat. Eat meat in moderation.
- Vegetables: Focus on eating vegetables that grow above the ground, mainly leafy green vegetables.
- Dairy: Buy full-fat dairy products.
- Nuts and seeds: Eat fat-rich nuts such as macadamia and almonds.
- Beverages: Stick to drinking mostly water. You can flavor it with lemon or lime juice and stevia-based flavorings.

Let's discuss this in detail.

Fats and Oils

- Saturated fats: consume lard, coconut oil, ghee, and butter.
- Monounsaturated fats: avocado, olive, and macadamia nut oils.
- Polyunsaturated fats: Eat naturally produced polyunsaturated fats from foods such as fatty fish and animal protein. Avoid processed polyunsaturated fat such as margarine spreads.
- Trans fats: Completely avoid.

Protein

Here are the best proteins for you

- Fish: Wild-caught fish like trout, snapper, salmon, mackerel, halibut, cod, tuna, catfish — fattier fish are better
- Shellfish: Mussels, squid, scallops, crab, lobster, oysters, clams
- Whole eggs: Free-range from the local market
- Beef: Fatty cuts of steak, stew meat, roasts, ground beef
- Pork: Ham, tenderloin, pork chops, pork loin, ground beef
- Poultry: Wild game, chicken, quail, pheasant, duck

- Offal/Organ: Tongue, kidney, liver, heart
- Other meat: Wild game, turkey, veal, lamb, goat
- Bacon and sausage: Avoid sugar or extra filler added items
- Nut butter: Natural, unsweetened made from fattier nuts like macadamia or almond

Vegetables and Fruit

Eat mostly vegetables that are low in carbs and high in nutrients. Focus on cruciferous vegetables that are leafy, green, and grown above ground.

Limit the vegetables and fruits listed below:

- Nightshades: peppers, eggplant, tomatoes
- Root vegetables: Squash, mushrooms, garlic, parsnips, onions
- Berries: Blueberries, blackberries, raspberries
- Citrus: Oranges, lemons, limes
- Starchy fruits and vegetables: Bananas, potatoes

Dairy Products

Here are some examples of dairy you can eat on a Keto diet:

- Hard cheeses, including Swiss, Parmesan, feta, aged cheddar

- Soft cheeses, including Monterey Jack, Colby, blue, brie, mozzarella
- Spreadable cheeses, including crème Fraîche, mascarpone, sour cream, cream cheese, cottage cheese
- Homemade mayonnaise
- Heavy whipping cream
- Greek yogurt

Nuts and Seeds

- Low carb, fat-rich nuts: Pecans, Brazil nuts, macadamia nuts
- Moderate carb, fat-rich nuts: Peanuts, hazelnuts, almonds, walnuts, pine nuts
- High carb nuts: Avoid cashews and pistachios

Water and Beverages

Here is a list of beverages that the Keto diet allows:

- Water: Drink more than eight glasses of water daily
- Broth: Broth is important for Keto dieters. It is loaded with vitamins and nutrients and helps to replace electrolytes.
- Tea and coffee
- Unsweetened almond and coconut milks
- Sweeteners such as stevia and sucralose are fine
- Avoid or severely reduce diet soda

- Hard liquor (avoid beer and wine because of high carb content

Spices

Cayenne Pepper	Chili Powder
Cinnamon	Cumin
Oregano	Basil
Cilantro	Parsley
Rosemary	Thyme

Condiments and Sauces

Keto-friendly condiments include:

- Syrups flavored with acceptable sweeteners
- Unsweetened, fatty salad dressings
- Worcestershire sauce
- Horseradish
- Low- or no-sugar added relish
- Low- or no-sugar added sauerkraut
- Cage-free mayonnaise
- Hot sauce
- Mustard
- Low- or no-sugar added ketchup

Try to avoid pre-made condiments

Sweeteners

Keto recommended sweeteners:

- Stevia
- Sucralose
- Erythritol
- Monk fruit
- Xylitol, in moderation

Foods to avoid

- Sugar: Typically found in ice cream, chocolate, candy, sports drinks, juice, and soda. Avoid sugar completely.
- Grains: Avoid bread, buns, rice, corn, pastries, cake, cereal, pasta, and beer. Avoid whole grains, including quinoa, buckwheat, barley, rye, and wheat.
- Starch: Avoid vegetables like yams and potatoes and other foods like muesli and oats.
- Trans fats: Avoid them completely.
- Fruit: Avoid fruits that are high in sugar (bananas, oranges, and apples)
- Low-fat foods: Low-fat foods are high in carbs and sugar. Avoid them.

Health Benefits of Ketogenic Diet

The Ketogenic diet is great for losing weight and is one of the healthiest diets available. Let's discuss the scientifically proven health benefits of this diet:

1. Increases your good cholesterol levels and decreases bad cholesterol levels: The diet increases your HDL or good cholesterol. Study shows (http://europepmc. org/abstract/MED/11374850/reload=0;jsessionid= 3xh9AgWu71C5wgBypxTn.0) that increased good cholesterol levels lowers your risk of heart disease. Another study also shows (https://academic.oup.com/ ajcn/article/77/5/1146/4689813) including that more fat in your diet is one of the best ways to increase your good cholesterol levels. Another study shows ((https:// academic.oup.com/jn/article/136/2/384/4664306) that eating a low-carb diet lowers bad (LDL) cholesterol in your bloodstream.

2. Lowers the amount of fat molecules in your bloodstream: Your blood pressure, HDL, LDL, and fat molecules in the bloodstream (triglycerides) jointly increase or decrease your risk of heart disease. You may think eating more fat would increase the amount of fat molecules in your bloodstream, but it is not the case. Study shows (https://www.ncbi.nlm.nih.gov/ pubmed/20107198) that eating a low-carb diet can lower your triglyceride levels.

3. Lowers your blood pressure: The good news is the Ketogenic diet can lower your blood pressure. High blood pressure can trigger heart disease and increase your risk of stroke or kidney failure. Recent data provided by the CDC show that approximately 30% of Americans suffer from high blood pressure. The study shows (https://academic.oup.com/jcem/article/89/6/2717/2870310) that a low-carb diet can lower your high blood pressure and decrease your risk for related diseases.

4. Lowers your risk of diabetes: Insulin is an important hormone in your body. You develop diabetes when your body develops insulin resistance. Many studies show that eating a high-carb diet causes diabetes because carbs break down quickly in the body and cause a blood sugar spike. If this energy/glucose is not used up, it gets stored as fat cells. With a low-carb diet, you eat fewer carbs, so your body processes less glucose, which is why the Ketogenic diet is excellent for controlling type 2 diabetes. (https://nutritionandmetabolism.biomedcentral.com/articles/10.1186/1743-7075-5-10, https://www.ncbi.nlm.nih.gov/pmc/articles/PMC2633336/).

5. Helps you lose weight: The Ketogenic diet can help you control your insulin levels, which means that the diet is perfect for losing weight (https://www.nejm.org/doi/full/10.1056/NEJMoa022637). Importantly,

the diet can help you lose dangerous abdominal fat. The abdominal, or belly fat, triggers insulin resistance and other chronic diseases. Following the Ketogenic diet will give you both short-term and long-term weight loss benefits and boost overall health. (https://www.nejm.org/doi/full/10.1056/NEJMoa022207).

6. Fights metabolic syndrome: Metabolic syndrome is a set of risk factors. Jointly they can increase your risk of diabetes, heart disease, and stroke. Health experts recommend treating MS through lifestyle changes. Staring a low-carb diet can lower your risk of MS.

7. Naturally lowers your appetite: Inability to control your appetite and hunger is one reason for weight gain. The Ketogenic diet reduces your appetite and helps you lose weight. Study shows (https://www.ncbi.nlm.nih.gov/pubmed/17228046) that a low-carb diet can naturally reduce hunger. Sugar is one of the addictive foods. With a high-carb diet, you eat many sugar and sugar-based foods, which only causes you to eat more sugar-rich foods. A low-carb Ketogenic diet prohibits sugar consumption and lowers your appetite.

8. Boosts your mood: Mood disorders, such as anxiety and depression, are one of the major causes of low productivity. They also lower your quality of life and relationships with loved ones. This study shows (https://www.ncbi.nlm.nih.gov/pubmed/17228046) that a low-carb diet can also boost your mood.

Key benefits of using an air fryer for cooking while on the Ketogenic diet

1. The ketogenic diet is a high-fat, moderate-protein, and low-carb diet. You can achieve your diet goals by using an air fryer for cooking your meals.
2. You can use keto-recommended fats for cooking protein dishes in the air fryer.
3. You have to avoid carb-rich foods when following the keto diet. The air fryer helps you cook tasty Keto meals that are low in carbs.
4. Eating enough protein and continuing with the Keto diet can be a problem for some. The air fryer makes cooking protein easier and helps you to stay with the diet plan.

THE VEGAN DIET

The vegan lifestyle is becoming popular these days. The diet is also called a plant-based diet. Vegans do not eat any food derived from animal sources, including poultry, red meat, eggs, dairy, and honey. People who follow a vegan diet often see vegan as a lifestyle rather than just a way of eating. They also avoid animal products such as fur, leather, or any other clothing item. People choose to be vegan for many reasons, including animal rights, health, and the environment.

Types of vegetarian diets

1. Vegan: No animal products, no honey, no leather products
2. Lacto-Ovo-Vegetarian: Includes eggs and dairy
3. Lacto-vegetarian: Includes dairy
4. Ovo-vegetarian: Includes eggs
5. Flexitarian: Includes meat or poultry, occasionally
6. Pescatarian: Includes shellfish and/or fish

Foods to eat on a vegan diet

- Vegetables
- Fruits
- Grains
- Beans
- Seeds
- Nuts
- Herbs & spices

Top vegan swaps

- Milk > Almond milk
- Cream > Coconut cream
- Butter > Olive oil
- Cheese > Nutritional yeast
- Eggs > Flax egg

Top vegan protein

- Tempeh
- Chickpeas
- Soybeans
- Tofu
- Lentils
- Quinoa
- Black beans
- Peanut butter
- Kidney beans
- Almonds
- Veggie burgers
- Pumpkin seeds

The Benefits of a Vegan Diet

Becoming a vegan is not a simple dietary choice. Veganism is a philosophy and a lifestyle choice. A vegan avoids eating anything of animal origin, and they don't use any animal-based clothes or products. Here are the benefits of a vegan diet:

1. You will stay disease-free: Various studies show that a vegan diet is healthier than the standard American diet. It is especially helpful in preventing, treating, or even reversing high blood pressure and heart disease as well as lowering the risk of cancer.

2. You will lose weight: The standard American diet is

low in complex carbohydrates and plant-based foods and high in saturated fats and processed foods. Eating this diet is making you fat and killing you slowly. According to the CDC, 15% of children and 64% of adults in the U.S. are overweight and are at risk of weight-related diseases such as heart disease, diabetes, and stroke. A recent study shows that a vegetarian diet helps people lose an average of 24 pounds in the first year, and dieters continue to lose weight as long as they stay on a vegan diet.

3. You will live longer: According to Michael F. Roizen, MD, the author of *The RealAge Diet*, switching from the standard American diet to a vegan diet will add up to 13 years to your life. Studies show that people who eat more saturated fat have a shorter life span because animal products lower your energy, clog your arteries, and slow down your immune system.

4. The vegan diet will give you more energy: Eating the usual American diet means excessive fat is in your bloodstream. This additional unhealthy fat means your veins will be narrower and your body tissues won't get sufficient oxygen. As a result, you will feel tired and sluggish. On the other hand, a balanced vegan diet is naturally free of artery-clogging animal products that make you slow and sluggish. Furthermore, vegan foods – whole grains, vegetables, legumes, and fruits — are high in complex carbohydrates and provide your body

enough energizing fuel. Vegetarian foods also contain a lot of fiber, which helps eliminate waste from your body and keeps you healthy and energetic.

5. You will lower pollution: According to the U.S. Environmental Protection Agency, animal waste and chemical runoff from factory farms are responsible for stream and river water pollution. Runoff from farmlands has become one of the greatest threats to water quality.

6. You will help prevent famine: Recent data show that 70% of the grains produced in the U.S. are used to feed animals raised for meat. This amount of grain can feed approximately 800 million people across the world. So go vegan and encourage others to join you. This could help prevent famine.

7. You save money: Data shows that an average American spends 10% of their food budget buying meat. The following report shows that you could save $750 a year by going vegan. https://www.huffingtonpost.ca/2015/10/15/vegetarian-diet-cost_n_8306172.html

8. You will enjoy it: The last reason you should go vegan is that the diet is delicious. These days the demand for vegan foods has increased, and food companies are introducing more delicious meat and dairy product alternatives that are healthier and taste like the real thing.

Key benefits of using an air fryer for cooking while on the Vegan diet

1. The vegan diet can become boring for some. You can use the air fryer to cook a variety of tasty vegan dishes and make the vegan diet interesting.

2. The vegan diet is mostly plant-based. Traditionally cooking plant-based foods can make the diet plan hard to follow. Using the air fryer to make plant-based foods is enjoyable.

3. Some people miss the taste of meat when they follow the vegan diet. You can use the air fryer to cook vegan foods with spices, so you feel as if you are eating meat dishes without actually eating meat.

4. One of the main benefits of the vegan diet is that you lose weight with this diet. However, using too much oil can make it hard for you to lose weight. The air fryer helps you to use less oil and achieve your weight loss goals with the vegan diet.

CONCLUSION

This is a comprehensive air fryer usage, buying, safety, and maintenance guide. The first chapter familiarizes you with the air fryer. It is a relatively new appliance that uses Rapid Air Technology. An air fryer is similar to a countertop convection oven, but works even better. It is a simple appliance with a base, basket, and basket base. You can use the air fryer to cook a variety of foods.

Using an air fryer gives you a variety of benefits. You use less energy and oil, which means healthier food for you quickly. The appliance is great for frozen foods and easy to clean. Automatic cooking functions mean no guesswork when cooking. You need various accessories to cook different foods in the air fryer. Accessories include the cake barrel, grill pan, rack, pizza pan, silicone liners, oil sprayers, Bundt pans, ramekins, parchment paper liners, instant meat and food thermometer, French fry cutter, and more.

Before using your air fryer, you need to understand the appliance well. You need to know a variety of things, including cooking times, minimum temperatures, how to cook in batches, and how to avoid smoking. As a beginner user, you need solid information to use your air fryer wisely. You should use parchment paper for easy cleanup. Drain excess fat, preheat the air fryer before cooking, shake the basket, and use a baking pan for breaded foods.

An air fryer is more advanced than a deep fryer or an oven. Unlike a deep fryer, you don't have to use a huge amount of oil in the air fryer. This gives you healthier food. The sleek design of an air fryer makes it easier to clean. When cooking in a convection oven, you often have to fry the food for a few minutes before you put it in the oven. However, you don't have to follow this step with an air fryer.

A microwave oven can cook foods quickly, but you will get more flavorful foods with an air fryer. A pressure cooker helps you cook meals, but you won't get crispy fried foods. You can often make mistakes when using an air fryer. For example, you need to check your food often when cooking in the air fryer. When you start to use an air fryer, you will need to check the food several times during cooking to be sure to avoid beginner mistakes such as overcrowding the basket, not patting your proteins dry, not cleaning the air fryer properly, and not using the air fryer for baking.

Besides cooking, your air fryer can be used for other things: as a proof box, to steam foods, as a meatloaf pan, for slow cooking, and more. Air fryers cook a bit differently than an oven, so you can't use traditional oven recipes. You need to adjust the temperature and time a little bit.

The second chapter discusses the details of different models of air fryers available in the market. The price of air fryers ranges from $50 to $300. You can find 2-quart, 5-quart, 8-quart, and even 20-quart (air fryer plus convection oven) air fryers in the market. There are mainly three types available: basket type, paddle-style, and countertop convection oven. When buying an air fryer, you need to look at capacity, wattage, temperature range, and safety.

If you are looking for a basket-type air fryer, you can buy a Philips air fryer or GoWISE air fryer (cheaper). If you want the functions of both a convection oven and an air fryer, then go for Cuisinart air fryer convection toaster oven, Ninja Foodi 8-in-1 Toaster Oven and Air Fryer, Breville Smart Oven Air, or Power XL Air Fryer Pro.

If you have a big family, you can use Iconites 10-in-1 Air Fryer Oven, 20-Quart Air Fryer Toaster Oven Combo, Greek Chef Air Fryer Toaster Oven, or the Kalorik 26-Quart Digital Maxx Air Fryer Oven. You need a variety of accessories with an air fryer, including a grill pan, air fryer liners, rack, oil sprayer, heat resistant tongs, silicone cups, and others.

Chapter three discusses how you to set up your air fryer. First, you need to place your appliance on an even surface and make sure there are at least 5 inches of space between the air fryer and the wall. Read the manual carefully. Each model and brand are a bit different than the others. When using the air fryer for the first time, use a vinegar and lemon juice mixture to remove the plastic odor from the air fryer.

The beginner air fryer tips are important for first-time air fryer users. Buying the right size air fryer is important. If you have a small family, then a 3.7 quart or smaller air fryer is fine. You need 5.8 quarts or larger for a family of 3 or more. It is important to clean your air fryer after each use. Avoid aerosol sprays and use bottled oil sprayers. Don't overcrowd the basket and use a toothpick to hold light foods in place. If you notice smoke rising from the air fryer during cooking, you need to stop and open the door to investigate what is causing it.

Chapter four is all about using your air fryer correctly. All air fryers come with warning cards and warning labels. Read them carefully. Remove the air fryer from the packaging box and place it on a kitchen countertop next to a power outlet. Clean the removable parts and remove the plastic odor according to the method described in this book. Then follow recipe instructions to cook your food.

The Dos and Don'ts section of this chapter is important. You need to know what you can and cannot do with your air fryer. The tricks sections also give you some valuable tips. Detailed air fryer cooking charts give you a comprehensive idea of food quantity, time, and temperature. The notes section tells you if and when you have to flip the food or shake the basket. The last part of the chapter includes measurement conversions, an oven temperature chart, and an air fryer recipe converter website.

Chapter five discusses caring for and maintaining the air fryer. The control dials show you how to operate an air fryer. Cleaning an air fryer is not difficult. You should clean the air fryer after every use. Allow the air fryer to cool, then wash the removable parts with a wet sponge or a soft cloth using hot soapy water to clean them. Then use a damp cloth to wipe down the insides, heating element, and outside of the air fryer.

Sometimes food gets stuck on the air fryer basket. In this situation, you need to soak the basket in hot soapy water for a few minutes, then scrub with a damp microfiber cloth to clean. If you do not need your air fryer for a few days, you should clean it and store it in a cabinet. You have to check the air fryer cord regularly. If you notice any damage, then take the appliance to electrician. There are a few safety tips you need to follow. For example, do not buy a cheap, low-quality air fryer. Always place the air fryer on an even surface and read the manual. Chapter six discusses frequently asked questions.

After buying your air fryer, you may face a variety of problems. For example, your air fryer doesn't turn on. It can happen because of a variety of reasons. White or black smoke coming out of your air fryer can be annoying. You must remove the plastic smell before using the air fryer for the first time. Food not cooking perfectly or cooking unevenly is a frustrating problem. This chapter provides all the solutions for air fryer problems and more.

The last chapter discusses air fryers and various diet plans.

LEAVE A 1-CLICK REVIEW!

Customer reviews

★★★★★ 5 out of 5

2 global ratings

5 star		100%
4 star		0%
3 star		0%
2 star		0%
1 star		0%

Review this product

Share your thoughts with other customers

> Write a customer review

I would be incredibly thankful if you could take just 60 seconds to write a brief review on Amazon, even if it's just a few sentences!

Scan QR code to leave a review!

REFERENCE

Xie, J. (2021, Mar. 16). *Everything You Need To Know About Your Air Fryer.* Delish. https://www.delish.com/cooking/a35600230/what-is-an-air-fryer/

Do Air Fryers Have Health Benefits? (2019, Aug. 27). WebMD. https://www.webmd.com/food-recipes/air-fryers

How Do Air Fryers Work and Do They Live Up to the Hype? (2019, Oct. 23). The Spruce Eats. https://www.thespruceeats.com/how-does-an-air-fryer-work-4693673

Price, M. (2021, Jan. 26). *Air fryer vs. oven baking: What's the best way to cook?* CNET. https://www.cnet.com/home/kitchen-and-household/air-fryer-vs-oven-baking-which-is-better-way-cook-frying-wings-fryer/

Kitchens, T. (2018, Oct. 24). *How to Use an Air Fryer*. Tablespoon.Com. https://www.tablespoon.com/meals/how-to-use-an-air-fryer

Laurence, Meredith. "Bacon Blue Burger." *Blue Jean Chef — Meredith Laurence*, 19 May 2020, bluejeanchef.com/cooking-school/air-frying-101

"Air Fryer 101." *Dummies*, 13 May 2020, www.dummies.com/food-drink/cooking/air-fryer-101

"Air Frying: The Basics & Need-to-Know." *Metabolic Research Center*, 20 Dec. 2020, www.emetabolic.com/blog/eat-well/air-frying-the-basics-need-to-know

NewAir. "Air Fryer 101: Your Answers to Oil-Less Cooking." *NewAir*, 1 May 2019, www.newair.com/blogs/learn/air-fryer-101-your-answers-to-oil-less-cooking

Box, Best Recipe. "What Is Air Frying? And Easy Recipe ECookbooks." *Best Recipe Box*, 4 Feb. 2021, bestrecipebox.com/what-is-air-frying

Sarah. "Best Air Fryers of 2021." *Live Eat Learn*, 8 Jan. 2021, www.liveeatlearn.com/best-air-fryers

Nicole Papantoniou, Good Housekeeping Institute. "9 Best Air Fryers of 2021, According to Kitchen Appliance Pros." *Good Housekeeping*, 11 Nov. 2020, www.goodhousekeeping.com/appliances/a24630295/best-air-fryers-reviews

The Editors. "The Best Air Fryers on Amazon, According to Hyperenthusiastic Reviewers." *The Strategist*, 4 Jan. 2021, nymag.com/strategist/article/best-air-fryers.html

Bennett, Brian. "Best Air Fryer for 2021: Ninja, Philips, Dash, Cosori, and More." *CNET*, 17 Mar. 2021, www.cnet.com/home/kitchen-and-household/best-air-fryer

Williams, Leah. "Quick Review: The Philips Airfryer XXL Is an Absolute Dreamboat." *Lifehacker Australia*, 26 Oct. 2020, www.lifehacker.com.au/2020/10/philips-airfryer-xxl-air-fryer-review/#:%7E:text=The%20Philips%20Airfry-er%20XXL%20is%20so%20easy%20to%20use%2C%20it,mod-el%20is%20another%20attractive%20feature

---. "Philips Airfryer XXL Review: Big Portions Can't Redeem This Air Fryer." *CNET*, 29 Apr. 2018, www.cnet.com/re-views/philips-airfryer-xxl-review

MargaretC. "Real Gowise 5.8qt Air Fryer Review [Bacon, Curly Fries, Brussel Sprouts]." *Healthy But Smart*, 15 Apr. 2021, healthybutsmart.com/gowise-air-fryer-review

Ro, Lauren. "This Compact, Do-It-All Oven Makes Me Feel Like Julia Child in Quarantine." *The Strategist*, 21 July 2020, nymag.com/strategist/article/cuisinart-air-fryer-toaster-oven.html

healthyew. "T-Fal ActiFry Review: '2 Things You Can't Do with Other Fryers.'" *Healthy But Smart*, 15 Apr. 2021, healthybutsmart.com/t-fal-fz7002-actifry-review

---. "T-Fal FZ7002 Actifry Review: Even Superb Fries Don't Make This Air Fryer a Good Deal." *CNET*, 29 Apr. 2018, www.cnet.com/reviews/t-fal-actifry-fz7002-review

---. "Black & Decker Purifry Review: This Air Fryer Costs Less, but Cooks Less Too." *CNET*, 28 Feb. 2018, www.cnet.com/reviews/black-decker-purifry-review

PCMag. "Cosori Smart 5.8-Quart Air Fryer Review." *PCMAG*, 5 Mar. 2021, www.pcmag.com/reviews/cosori-smart-58-quart-air-fryer

Staysnatched. "Cosori Air Fryer Honest Review." *Stay Snatched*, 10 Nov. 2019, www.staysnatched.com/cosori-air-fryer-review

Price, Molly. "Instant Vortex Plus Review: This 7-in-1 Air Fryer Feels Undercooked." *CNET*, 25 July 2019, www.cnet.com/reviews/instant-pot-vortex-plus-air-fryer-review-review

"Instant Vortex Plus 7-in-1 Air Fryer Oven Review." *The Spruce Eats*, 15 Jan. 2020, www.thespruceeats.com/instant-vortex-plus-7-in-1-air-fryer-oven-review-4782099

Cookandbrown. "Ninja Air Fryer Max XL Reviews: Read before Buying." *Cook and Brown,* 15 Nov. 2020, cookandbrown.com/ninja-air-fryer-max-xl-reviews

Admin. "Ninja Air Fryer That Cooks, Crisps and Dehydrates, with 4 Quart Capacity, and a High Gloss Finish [Review]." *Confirm Reviews,* 30 Mar. 2021, www.confirmreviews.com/ninja-air-fryer

Ogden, Rachel. "Ninja Air Fryer Max AF160UK." *Trusted Reviews,* 6 Dec. 2019, www.trustedreviews.com/reviews/ninja-air-fryer-max-af160uk

"Chefman 3.5-Liter Matte Digital TurboFry Air Fryer Review." *The Spruce Eats,* 5 Jan. 2021, www.thespruceeats.com/chefman-turbofry-air-fryer-review-5080587

---. "The 2 Best Chefman Air Fryers Reviewed & Compared [11 Photos]." *Healthy But Smart,* 15 Apr. 2021, healthybutsmart.com/chefman-air-fryer-review

H, Victoria. "PowerXL Air Fryer Pro Review." *Giveaways 4 Mom,* 8 Jan. 2020, giveaways4mom.com/powerxl-air-fryer-pro-review

Hbs-Review-Team. "'Woah That Cooked Fast!': My Power Air Fryer Oven Review." *Healthy But Smart,* 15 Apr. 2021, healthybutsmart.com/power-airfryer-oven-review

Tkarlilar. "GoWISE USA GW22955 7-Quart Air Fryer with Dehydrator Review | Just New Releases." *Just New Releases |,* 1

Dec. 2019, justnewreleases.com/gowise-usa-gw22955-7-quart-air-fryer-with-dehydrator-review

Zone, Home Cooking. "The Best Air Fryer For A Large Family." *Homecookingzone.Com*, 7 May 2020, homecookingzone.com/best-air-fryer-for-large-family

Smythe, Jayne, and Jayne Smythe. "DASH Air Fryer...Would I Buy It Again? | In-Depth Review | Air Fryers." *Dutch Ovens & Cookware*, 21 Jan. 2020, www.dutchovenscookware.com/dash-air-fryer

"Dash Compact Air Fryer Review." *The Spruce Eats*, 15 Jan. 2020, www.thespruceeats.com/dash-compact-air-fryer-review-4782094

Pitre, Urvashi. "Gourmia Air Fryer Review — Is The Gourmia Right For You?" *Wouldibuythis.Com*, 15 Feb. 2021, wouldibuythis.com/gourmia-air-fryer-review

Wilkins, Darrian. "Gourmia Air Fryer Reviews." *KitchenFold*, 11 Sep. 2020, kitchenfold.com/air-fryers/gourmia-air-fryer-reviews

Rich. "Ninja Foodi Air Fryer Oven Reviews for 2021." *Meal Prepify*, 29 Mar. 2021, mealprepify.com/ninja-foodi-air-fryer-oven-reviews

Jamie. "Chefman Air Fryer Reviews: Top Models Compared." *Daring Kitchen*, 11 Feb. 2021, thedaringkitchen.com/chefman-air-fryer-reviews

"Bella Air Fryer Review: 2.6QT and 5.3QT, Which One to Buy?" *Fryer Consumer,* 1 Apr. 2021, fryerconsumer.com/reviews/bella-air-fryer

"Emeril Lagasse Power AirFryer 360 Review." *The Spruce Eats,* 11 Mar. 2021, www.thespruceeats.com/emeril-lagasse-power-airfryer-360-review-5078324

Laurence, Meredith. (2020, June 11). "Blueberry Blondies." *Blue Jean Chef — Meredith Laurence.* https://bluejeanchef.com/cooking-school/how-to-choose-an-air-fryer/

Air Fryer 101. (2020, May 13). Dummies. https://www.dummies.com/food-drink/cooking/air-fryer-101/

Box, B. R. (2021, Feb. 4). *What is Air Frying? and Easy Recipe eCookbooks.* Best Recipe Box. https://bestrecipebox.com/what-is-air-frying/

Thurrott, S. (2020, July 7). *Air fryer guide: How air frying works and the best recipes.* NBC News. https://www.nbcnews.com/better/lifestyle/best-air-fryers-recipes-ncna1114616

How To Use an Air Fryer: A First-Timer's Guide. (2021, Feb. 10). Simply Recipes. https://www.simplyrecipes.com/how_to_use_an_air_fryer_a_first_timers_guide/

Broida, R. (2019, Apr. 16). *7 tips for using an air fryer.* CNET. https://www.cnet.com/home/kitchen-and-household/tips-for-using-an-air-fryer/

Pan, J. (2021, Jan. 15). *Here's What the Buttons on Your Air Fryer Actually Mean*. Taste of Home. https://www.tasteofhome.com/article/how-to-use-air-fryer/

B. (2021, Mar. 30). *17 Air Fryer Tips for Better Air Frying*. Recipes From A Pantry. https://recipesfromapantry.com/air-fryer-tips/

How To Use an Air Fryer: A First-Timer's Guide. (2021, Feb. 21). Simply Recipes. https://www.simplyrecipes.com/how_to_use_an_air_fryer_a_first_timers_guide/

L. (2021, Jan. 13). *5 Best Foods to Reheat in the Air Fryer | Reheating Leftovers is Easy*. Hip2Save. https://hip2save.com/tips/reheating-leftovers-in-an-air-fryer/

How To Reheat Food In An Airfryer + The Leftovers To Reheat! (2020, Dec. 11). Apelka. https://mybudgetrecipes.com/how-to-reheat-food-in-an-airfryer/

How To Use an Air Fryer: A First-Timer's Guide. (2021, Feb. 10). Simply Recipes. https://www.simplyrecipes.com/how_to_use_an_air_fryer_a_first_timers_guide/

Nicole Papantoniou, Good Housekeeping Institute. (2021, Mar. 19). *Everything You Need to Know About Air Fryers*. Good Housekeeping. https://www.goodhousekeeping.com/appliances/a28436830/what-is-an-air-fryer/

Thurrott, S. (2020, July 7). *Air fryer guide: How air frying works and the best recipes.* NBC News. https://www.nbcnews.com/better/lifestyle/best-air-fryers-recipes-ncna1114616

Box, B. R. (2021, Feb. 4). *What is Air Frying? and Easy Recipe eCookbooks.* Best Recipe Box. https://bestrecipebox.com/what-is-air-frying/

Szewczyk, J. (2020, Sep. 16). *18 Air Fryer Tricks You Should Know About.* BuzzFeed. https://www.buzzfeed.com/jesseszewczyk/air-fryer-tips-tricks

Reference

NewAir. (2019, May 1). *Air Fryer 101: Your Answers to Oil-Less Cooking.* https://www.newair.com/blogs/learn/air-fryer-101-your-answers-to-oil-less-cooking

Answers to All of Your Air Fryer Questions. (2020, Feb. 12). Air Frying. https://www.americastestkitchen.com/guides/air-frying/frequently-asked-air-frying-questions

NewAir. (2019, May 1). *Air Fryer Cleaning & Maintenance.* https://www.newair.com/blogs/learn/air-fryer-cleaning-maintenance

Best Practices for Air Fryer Cleaning and Maintenance. (2020, Feb. 11). Airfryer.Net. https://airfryer.net/cleaning-the-air-fryer

NewAir. (2019, May 1). *Air Fryer 101: Your Answers to Oil-Less Cooking.* https://www.newair.com/blogs/learn/air-fryer-101-your-answers-to-oil-less-cooking

Answers to All of Your Air Fryer Questions. (2020, Jan. 12). Air Frying. https://www.americastestkitchen.com/guides/air-frying/frequently-asked-air-frying-questions

E. (2021, Mar. 8). *Air Fryer Keeps Turning Off: How to Fix.* Ready To DIY. https://readytodiy.com/air-fryer-keeps-turning-off-how-to-fix-0051/

Rector, C. P. (2021, Feb.14). *Air Fryer Problems and Solutions! Easy Guide [With Image].* Best Fryer Review. https://www.fryerly.com/how-to-troubleshoot-air-fryer-problems/

Air Fryer 101 and Recipes to Try. (2021, Apr. 9). Forks Over Knives. https://www.forksoverknives.com/how-tos/air-fryer-101-how-to-use-plus-recipes/

Nicole Papantoniou, Good Housekeeping Institute. (2021, Mar. 19). *Everything You Need to Know About Air Fryers.* Good Housekeeping. https://www.goodhousekeeping.com/appliances/a28436830/what-is-an-air-fryer/

Thurrott, S. (2020, July 7). *Air fryer guide: How air frying works and the best recipes.* NBC News. https://www.nbcnews.com/better/lifestyle/best-air-fryers-recipes-ncna1114616

S. (2020, Dec. 23). *5 Basics of The Mediterranean Lifestyle: A Mediterranean Girl's Perspective*. The Mediterranean Dish. https://www.themediterraneandish.com/5-basics-mediterranean-lifestyle-mediterranean-girls-perspective/

The Mediterranean Lifestyle-7 Principles of the Mediterranean Lifestyle. (2020, Feb. 11). The Mediterranean Lifestyle. https://www.themediterraneanlifestyle.co/7-principles

Beckenham, L. (2021, Jan. 26). *In Search of the Mediterranean Lifestyle*. Living on Mallorca. https://www.helencummins.com/mediterranean-lifestyle/

Contributor, M. (2019, May 13). *Living the Mediterranean Lifestyle*. American Society for Nutrition. https://nutrition.org/living-mediterranean-lifestyle/

Gunnars, K. B. (2018, July 24). *Mediterranean Diet 101: A Meal Plan and Beginner's Guide*. Healthline. https://www.healthline.com/nutrition/mediterranean-diet-meal-plan

NHS website. (2020, Dec. 30). *What is a Mediterranean diet?* Nhs.Uk. https://www.nhs.uk/live-well/eat-well/what-is-a-mediterranean-diet/#:%7E:text=The%20Mediterranean%20diet%20varies%20by,of%20meat%20and%20dairy%20foods

Mediterranean diet: A heart-healthy eating plan. (2019, June 21). Mayo Clinic. https://www.mayoclinic.org/healthy-

lifestyle/nutrition-and-healthy-eating/in-depth/
mediterranean-diet/art-20047801

M. (2021, Apr. 19). *The Mediterranean Diet.* HelpGuide.Org. https://www.helpguide.org/articles/diets/the-mediterranean-diet.htm

Salomon, S. H., & Kennedy, R. K. D. (2019, Mar. 19). *8 Scientific Health Benefits of the Mediterranean Diet | Everyday Health.* EverydayHealth.Com. https://www.everydayhealth.com/mediterranean-diet/scientific-health-benefits-mediterranean-diet/

12 Scientifically Proven Benefits of the Mediterranean Diet. (2020, Feb. 11). Verywell Fit. https://www.verywellfit.com/health-benefits-of-the-mediterranean-diet-4842600

Laurence, E. (2020, May 13). *9 Mediterranean Diet Benefits That Explain Why Experts Love It so Much.* Well+Good. https://www.wellandgood.com/mediterranean-diet-benefits/

What's a Ketogenic Diet? (2020, Feb. 12). WebMD. https://www.webmd.com/diet/ss/slideshow-ketogenic-diet

Eenfeldt, A., & Scher, B. (2021, Apr. 30). *A ketogenic diet for beginners.* Diet Doctor. https://www.dietdoctor.com/low-carb/keto

Clarke, C. (2021, Apr. 29). *What is the Keto Diet? [What to Eat, Tips, Recipes, FAQ]*. Ruled Me. https://www.ruled.me/guide-keto-diet/

Palinski-Wade, R. E. D., & Kennedy, R. K. D. (2020, Jan. 17). *What Is the Ketogenic Diet? Beginner's Guide, Food List, Sample Menu, and Scientific Review | Everyday Health*. EverydayHealth.Com. https://www.everydayhealth.com/diet-nutrition/ketogenic-diet/

The Basics of a Keto Diet and How It Works. (2020, Feb. 12). Verywell Fit. https://www.verywellfit.com/what-is-a-ketogenic-diet-2241628

KETO-MOJO. (2021, Feb. 15). *11 Health Benefits of the Ketogenic Diet*. https://keto-mojo.com/article/top-11-health-benefits-of-keto/

Clarke, C. (2019, Oct. 13). *The Benefits of The Ketogenic Diet*. Ruled Me. https://www.ruled.me/benefits-ketogenic-diet/

24 Benefits of the Ketogenic Diet. (2020, Dec. 2). Alexfergus.Com. https://www.alexfergus.com/blog/24-benefits-of-the-ketogenic-diet

B. (2021, Feb. 8). *20 Amazing Benefits of Keto Diet*. Castle in the Mountains. https://www.castleinthemountains.com/benefits-keto-diet/

Jockers. (2021, Feb. 24). *9 Proven Benefits of a Ketogenic Diet*. DrJockers.Com. https://drjockers.com/benefits-ketogenic-diet/

Watson, S. (2019, Oct. 2). *What Is a Vegan Diet?* WebMD. https://www.webmd.com/diet/vegan-diet-overview#1

Jhaveri, A. (2020, May 11). *A Beginner's Guide to Going Vegan and Living Your Best Plant-Based Life.* Greatist. https://greatist.com/eat/what-is-a-vegan-diet

Why go vegan? (2020, Dec. 21). The Vegan Society. https://www.vegansociety.com/go-vegan/why-go-vegan

Health Benefits of a Vegan Diet. (2020, Dec. 14). Rush University System for Health. https://www.rush.edu/news/health-benefits-vegan-diet

I Love Vegan. (2020, Nov. 14). *Benefits of a Vegan Lifestyle ».* https://www.ilovevegan.com/resources/benefits-of-a-vegan-lifestyle/

Webber, J. (2020, Dec. 15). *15 Vegan Lifestyle Benefits That Will Make You Never Look Back.* LIVEKINDLY. https://www.livekindly.co/vegan-lifestyle-benefits/